Zen in High Heels

Zen in High Heels

Find Your Way to
Personal Evolution and Peace
with Your Fabulousness Intact

Denise K. Evans

Life-Enhancing
Publishing

ZEN IN HIGH HEELS
Find Your Way to Personal Evolution and Peace with Your Fabulousness Intact

FIRST EDITION

ISBN 978-1-5445-4373-4 *Hardcover*

978-1-5445-4372-7 *Paperback*

978-1-5445-4374-1 *Ebook*

978-1-5445-4314-7 *Audiobook*

Contents

Introduction ix

Part I: Exploring the Dilemma 1

    1. The Struggle Is Real 3

    2. The Need for Zen 9

    3. The Journey: And So It Begins 19

Part II: Building Your Foundation 33

    4. ZEN Enemy #1 35

    5. Meditation 43

    6. Gratefulness 65

7. Intention..81

8. Words You Speak... 109

Part III: Navigating the Bumpy Road of Relationships 119

9. Personal Responsibility............................. 121

10. Non-Attachment 141

11. Relationships as Teachers 153

12. Relationships Continued........................... 161

Part IV: Tending to Your Vessel...175

13. Love Your Body...................................... 177

14. Nourish and Nurture............................... 201

Part V: Tying It All Together 221

15. Fluidity.. 223

16. The World Needs You.............................. 231

Conclusion 245

Recommended Reading................................. 251

This book is dedicated to

you

the reader.

If one sentence helps light your way for one moment,

one centimeter forward,

one degree of growth,

I rejoice.

And

to

Avery Faith-Maria,

my angel on Earth.

Introduction

*G*ot Zen? Is your zen MIA? Today was the perfect day to PICK up this book! How do I know? I know because the Universe offers tools, support and answers we seek as soon as our heart is open and our eyes are ready to see. A book filled with deep contemplation and guidance for spiritual growth found its way to your hands today.

Earlier in my life, I got the right grades, worked at the right job, drove the right car, and pursued the things you're "supposed" to pursue. I had most of what I thought I wanted. I went to church and considered myself a good person. But in quiet moments of solitude, there was a feeling that something was missing. I was longing for something more. I was not longing for more accomplishment or possessions, but instead, more meaning, more personal satisfaction.

I yearned for inner peace. A peace that would not be shaken by the ebb and flow of outside circumstances and influences. I experienced glimpses of that peace at times, after a particularly good night's sleep or during a deep-felt church sermon, perhaps, but those glimpses were easily disrupted and always fleeting.

I grew weary of constantly wondering, *What's next? When would I feel satisfaction that it's enough, that I'm doing enough? That I AM enough?* I wanted to feel a fullness and contentment about my life and within myself. Not fullness and contentment when *this* happens or *that* goes my way, but in the moment that is happening NOW. And why did this seem somehow elusive? Did I need to accomplish the next goal and hope that peace would find me then? Was peace waiting for me just around the corner? Or was I doing something wrong? I had an awareness that I wanted something more, but was not quite sure what that meant and absolutely no idea how to get there.

How could I stop focusing on all the external pressure—external measures of success—and get myself on to a path where joy and love and meaning could find me and express themselves in me and through me on a more regular basis? I wondered how I could get off the hamster wheel that my life felt like. I always felt like *after* I finish this laundry, clean out my closet, run these errands, fulfill family obligations, school or work assignments, pay off my car, *THEN* I will have time to make changes and figure out this nudging, nagging desire for something "more." But, as you know, the to-do list is never, ever fully checked off! Much to my dismay, it just continued to grow with more and more time-sucking tasks as weeks, months and years were ticking away.

My life wasn't that bad. I was not miserable, I just wanted to embody the mantras: "SEIZE THE DAY!," and "LIVE LIFE TO THE FULLEST!" *What would I need to change to actually live life like that?* I wondered.

It seemed to me like some religious leaders, people who practiced Eastern world philosophies, and some really old people I've met had found that sense of contentment I yearned for: a calm inner peace. They did not seem to be searching outside themselves for something in order to be happy.

I found myself questioning, *Is it possible to move toward this kind of enlightenment, toward a more evolved version of myself from right where I stand?* What about the mistakes I had made? What about the limitations I feel when I think about this daunting idea of spiritual growth? Would I be able to pursue personal expansion and experience that deep inner peace I was longing for, but still *enjoy* the life I had worked so hard to build? Could I enjoy the womanly traditions of wanting to look my best, wear lip gloss most of my waking moments, and dare I say it, even wear HIGH HEELS in conjunction with incorporating some time-honored practices for spiritual growth toward my very own personal zen? I want to experience zen, even if I choose to wear high heels—Yes! That is what I want! I want ZEN IN HIGH HEELS! And why not? What's wrong with that?

Seriously, to experience peace, harmony and meaning in my life, do I have to give up the things that bring me pleasure? So what if I am not a vegetarian? What if eating a Big Mac Extra Value Meal on occasion makes me feel blissful? Am I less deserving of inner peace than the guy next to me at yoga class who walked two miles to get there and whose shorts are made of 100% recycled milk cartons in reverence to the environment?

Is there not a place on the path to enlightenment for lip gloss and high heels? I was conflicted about this but determined to find out the answer! So with a pure heart, my quest for knowledge, or it would be more accurate to say my quest for WISDOM began.

This book has been inspired by my journey, the journey of so many women like you and I who really are making the effort to live our best life and reach our God-given potential. We are learning as we go, shining strong on some days, and failing miserably on other days as we strive for an "ideal" version of ourselves. A version of ourselves that somehow always remains just outside our reach in any given twenty-four-hour day.

Instead of a one-formula-fits-all approach, *Zen in High Heels* is meant to offer information and support. It is meant to help you engage on your journey of evolution, transformation, and potential, seeking a sense of peace, meaning and fulfillment without turning your back on the life that is yours now and the people who are part of it.

It is my desire that you feel validation that YOU are right where you are supposed to be! And know that WHERE YOU ARE today, there are choices available to you and time-tested tools for any of the ways you want to improve and add meaning to your life. Growth toward your soul's potential is always 100% of the time within reach.

Take the ideas that resonate with you and run with them. As for the ideas that pique your curiosity, or you think you disagree with, do your own research: investigate on your own to see if it is time to challenge a long-held belief. Maybe it is, maybe it is not—be open to the possibility.

In the large scheme of things, obviously, what brand of shoes you wear or how high the heel is are not important, but what IS actually important, truly invaluable, is to grow and experience a spectacular, fully evolving version of your Self on as many days as possible. YOU showing up for the people and experiences of your life: a gift only you, no other person ALIVE can give this world. Seize this day! Live your life to the fullest! Let's begin.

PART I

Exploring the Dilemma

CHAPTER 1

The Struggle Is Real

"Ask, and it shall be given unto you, seek and ye shall find."

—MATTHEW 7:11

*I*t is a good thing we are not born with a limit to the number of questions we can ask in a lifetime. Allow yourself to be curious, and with persistence, you will find the answers you seek. I speak from experience, as I began my journey with many questions. I needed to know: is it possible to achieve real peace and personal growth and move closer to my potential in all important aspects of life in a g-r-a-d-u-a-l way? Does it always come as a major epiphany or "light bulb" moment or with enormous sacrifice? Is true happiness possible without the latest designer purse or with less than 50,000 social media followers? Would being content in the here and now or attaining this inner peace I seek, deter me from having goals and aspirations for my future?

Can we fit deep and profound work to resolve our inner turmoil into our already busy, complicated lives? And does fully engaging on your spiritual path mean giving up the desire on the physical level to look and feel our best? Is enjoying some of the luxuries of the material world in and of itself contradictory to pursuing deeper meaning in life? Are squats, lunges, fashion, makeup and anti-aging efforts a waste of time and money? $90 night cream anyone? Or even worse, could these be barriers to spiritual growth? Can we seek zen while still wearing our high heels?

I yearned to know: is what ancient wisdom philosophers and traditions taught still true for us in the 21st century? Do the answers we seek actually lie within ourselves? Can't I Google, search YouTube, or download an app that will show me a shortcut to get my zen on? There must be a zen-producing hack by now!

Because commitment to deep spirituality and living at higher levels of consciousness is so often associated with people who make spiritual practice their life's calling and who are willing to give up material or what we consider to be pleasurable aspects of today's lifestyle, these questions are real, and therein lies the dilemma. I REALLY DO want to access my potential and my connection to the Divine on a more consistent basis. I REALLY DO want to be calm and grounded, living a life with more peace and less confusion. I want to live my life with more love, more meaning, more harmonious rela-tionships—but in a way that feels genuine and do-able for ME in the 21st century. After all, I still do have family, work, a social life, social media, dishes that need to be washed, obligations on my time and not-so-spiritual people to deal with!

Maybe you can relate? Perhaps professionally you've worked your way to the top. You are the badass boss—in the BEST way possible of course! In your pursuit of slaying it, you sacrificed and put all of your time and energy toward the career. To sustain that success however, you feel the need to keep putting that same level of dedica-tion into your work, struggling to find any balance in your life. Without a practice of inner nourishment, you will end up crashing and burn-ing, wondering why your relationships or your health are suffering. I am certain you want to figure out a way to have job satisfaction, the respect of your peers, the big paycheck, and also have the energy and understanding of how to carry that success with you to other parts of your life.

I would like to enjoy a glass of fine wine in the company of friends, a fabulous fitting pair of jeans, or a new pair of high heels without feeling I am abandoning my spiritual path. I am aware that there is much more to me than the way I look or the clothes I wear, but I want to know I can still enjoy these elements of my life! I'm certain I am not the only one who is grateful for the revelation that we can continue our climb up the corporate ladder, keep our high heels and still find our zen! We just have to keep perspective that such things are not the ultimate priority. We must not have the illusion that these things are somehow definitive in regard to our value in the world or in our meaning in life.

Zen in High Heels is really just a metaphor for engaging on your journey of evolution, transformation and potential, seeking a sense of peace, meaning and fulfillment without completely abandoning your current life. Most of us do not want to completely change all the components or cast aside all the people who make up our lives in pursuit of higher meaning and expanded spirituality. We want to figure out a way to incorporate growth and to actually enjoy our lives and the people who are a part of them MORE. We want to feel a sense of contentment on the daily, not just with the arrival of milestones like a graduation, promotion or wedding. We seek a sense of confidence, sans anxiety, with the direction we are heading.

It sounds like a lot of things to try to attain: higher meaning, expanded spirituality, contentment, confidence and connection, but these are all qualities you will experience and draw to you when you get honest and real about the deeper truth of who you are. When you find your zen, you will also find these virtues become more and more part of your everyday life. The zen we seek puts us on a path where we can actually be present in the moments and present with the people in our lives. When you engage more fully, you will feel more full. *This* is where true, genuine fulfillment comes from!

So the dilemma is this: how do I embrace spiritual truths taught long ago in a way that makes sense to *Me* today? In a way that will make a difference for *Me*? Not just theoretically—in a way that my mind can agree is true—but with practicality, in a way I can implement that would allow me to grow and experience lasting change and frequent zen? And why, oh WHY, does it seem so difficult?

I have been practicing the concepts I lay out in *Zen in High Heels* to achieve better relationships, better fitness, a clearer mind, less illness, a drama-free emotional life, and despite my natural "Type A" personality, substantial periods of inner peace! Inner peace that continues to appear more frequently and last for longer durations. Hallelujah! Can I get an amen?

I am the first with my hand up to admit that I am still a student of life. Still seeking, still growing, still not always getting it right. Like Joyce Meyer of Joyce Meyer Ministries says, "I may not be where I need to be, but THANK GOD I am not where I used to be!" Thank you Miss Joyce! Me too! I am not where I used to be; praise God!

For more than half of my life I have been on this quest for true health and wellness in mind, body and spirit. Years and years reading, studying, and integrating via trial and error everything I could find on these subjects. And although the information out there can seem overwhelming and often contradictory, I found that there are actually re-occurring themes and threads of truth that run consistent from the oldest philosophies to the newest "feel good" teachings. It is these commonalities around some key basic principles that have resonated with me and absolutely changed my life for the better.

After decades spent mustering through the teachings and wading in the deep, murky waters of spiritual principles, I might have saved a lot of time, confusion and frustration if I could have found such tools laid out in a way my 21st century mind could understand! It is my deepest intent that what you will find in these pages is exactly THAT. It is my truest desire that Zen in High Heels will serve as a bridge as you make your way.

There are some universal truths that applied long ago, and still apply today. Universal truths apply to me and they apply to you. They are indeed, Universal! As you will hear me say and come to know for yourself: TRUTH is TRUTH! And truth is always, ultimately, non-negotiable! Whether we accept it, or fight against it, truth remains what it is: TRUE! We must make the effort to know Universal truth principles and then apply them in the privacy of our heart, in our mind and in our day-to-day lives, to experience an expanded, more peaceful, more present version of ourselves. Let's continue.

CHAPTER 2

The Need for Zen

"Our days are simultaneously full to the bursting point and achingly, heartbreakingly empty."

—STEVEN PRESSFIELD

mericans are one of the most affluent and materially abundant people on Earth. Interestingly, I heard recently that we consume something like 74% of all prescription medication—antidepressants, antianxiety, blood pressure, sleeping medication, the list goes on. We are sick, worried, stressed and exhausted from not tending to our spirit, but instead, chasing the shiny ball. We seek material things, social status, fuller lips, whatever it is going to take to make us feel better. We will do almost anything to try to feel different than we actually really feel. We seek to gain approval; whether it is from our family, our social circle, or a broader internet based group of "friends" and "followers." Because attaining the approval we are seeking from others will certainly be the silencer of our woes; THEN, for sure, we will be happy and at peace. Right?

Actually, true happiness is a by-product found along the path as you seek your zen. Zen being peace: peace in your heart and in your mind. Zen being higher consciousness: an increased awareness about your life and about the human experience. Zen being enlightenment: clarity about who you are and what you are here to do. In the process of discovering your zen, you will gain that clarity. You will gain an understanding about what is truly important. Seeking and finding your zen puts you in alignment with what is important both in the long haul and also what is important for today, in *this* moment. We can see things in life from both a higher perspective and, at the same time, with deeper meaning. Actively pursuing your zen is what creates a happy and content soul and allows you to maneuver through life with so much more peace than you ever thought possible. Who wouldn't want to navigate life with more zen?

Most everyone these days is feeling busy and rushed, and overwhelmed, wondering why time is flying by. We are so busy planning this thing, that thing and the next thing, that we are not actually enjoying any of the things! Or if we manage to find enjoyment, it is fleeting, only to find ourselves back in the perpetual state of desire to get on to the next thing that is calling for our time and attention.

Overscheduling ourselves is not difficult in this media and social media-driven society. It's easy to look around and feel like we are not doing enough. No matter what we do, someone else is doing more, and doing it better. Thanks to social media platforms, we are no longer keeping up with the proverbial Jones'. We see composites of great qualities in other women, and most of the time, we just do not measure up. There is an overabundance of opportunity to feel inadequate. We are not quite good enough. In any given moment, we are just not enough.

We should be getting up at 5:00 a.m. and meditating for an hour, while somehow getting our recommended eight hours of sleep. We should be exercising six days a week: this week it's high-intensity training, last week was low-intensity training, next week they will say only yoga is best. We should be working on our PhD, or at least jumping through hoops to provide our pre-schooler an adequate education so they will be inclined to get theirs. We should be cooking every night with organic ingredients, but make sure you leave out the gluten! We should not have a wrinkle when we smile and God forbid you have a sunspot on your face...what is THAT doing THERE? I know I am not alone in observing this phenomenon. When is it ever going to be enough? Is true satisfaction with what IS, the way things actually ARE, in fact, elusive in this human experience?

This state of grasping to keep up puts most of us in survival mode on any given day. Even without realizing it, the subconscious is driving us around, putting our attention on everything that comes our way, whether it is meaningful or not. The incessant images and dialogue we ingest keep us simultaneously on high alert and in the numb zone. Always comparing, judging, blaming, reacting and overreacting, we survive on a mental diet of overstimulation of junk information that makes it very clear: you are not enough. You should be MORE.

The routine of our days is rote. The habit of clicking and checking and binging: a daily level of grind that is just enough—just enough distraction from what is calling for our expansion. Staying busy enough to keep ourselves from seeing what really matters. We may be surviving but not truly thriving.

Allowing ourselves to use distraction as our default mode of existence is a barrier to evolution. Busy-ness is the perfect decoy. It serves its purpose really; tricking us into believing we are doing things that eventually will lead to something meaningful. Staying busy is the socially acceptable norm. Hell, it's socially revered. "OMG, I am SOOOO busy!" Busy with this thing, that thing, the next thing, and really NO thing, that is to say nothing that really matters. When we are doing, doing, doing and going, going, going, we do not have time to BE; to BE with ourselves. There is no time to sit with a problem or issue, to create space for our deeper truth to come forward. Those secret desires we haven't yet acknowledged and that unhealed pain are just waiting for us to stop running from them. We find ourselves managing our schedule and putting out fires, rather than actually tending to and living our life.

There are definitely seasons of extra busyness: that deadline on a big project, the end of the school year for you, or your kids, holidays, etc.

But if that level of moving and pushing and grinding and tuning out your body and your mind to meet the outside demands of a schedule more than 300 days (arbitrary number) a year, it is time to take a closer look at your calendar and at *what is motivating you* to say YES to things that you know in your heart and soul are actually big fat NOs!

It's probably less relevant to talk about what is keeping us so busy on the daily, but more important that we all can agree on this critical point: our lives are too busy! We are in a chronic state of believing when _____ happens THEN we will be able to relax, be happy and get to that conversation, that creative project, or that situation the deeper part of us is tugging at us to get to. This is the lie of the century.

Zen is available in any moment. Not just "when" and "then." However, your zen will not be discovered in the chaos of an overly busy life. You will not find what you seek in the stress of running from here to there. Zen, no matter how bad you want it, can not be found in running yourself ragged due to neglecting your needs to make sure you don't disappoint everyone else! Zen is not found by trying to keep up with others or in the relentless pursuit of perfection or an unflawed version of yourself. There is nothing inherently wrong with striving to be your best or doing things for others. The anti-zen producing effects of these behaviors occur in our expectations of the benefit they will yield and in our underlying motivation.

Obsessing about our outward appearance and being preoccupied with what others think of us are two of the ways we attempt to disguise what lies underneath. We use our outward image as a veil to conceal what we want to keep hidden. Underneath the jokes, the designer clothes, the job title, the botox and the Instagram filters are all of the fears and insecurities and broken or neglected parts of you waiting for recognition and healing. But also underneath the outward facade are all of your deepest desires, hopes and dreams just waiting to be set free and realized.

You may be quite adept at hiding your truth from other people—but you cannot hide from your Self. Eventually it will catch up with you. And it is in your denial of that deeper truth, that misery will follow you. You cannot outrun what is inside you. New car? It's the same old you driving it. Extravagant vacation? Yep, it's the same restless mind, same body, same old familiar thoughts, same you sitting on that white sandy beach. New house? It's you waking up in that bed with the new fancy 1000 thread count sheets, feeling the exact same way you did before you moved in. Like the title of Jon Kabat-Zinn's book states so clearly: *Wherever You Go, There You Are!* Isn't that the truth?

So as we continue to think we will find happiness and what we are seeking *just on the other side* of achieving the next goal or getting the next level of material wealth, we actually find emptiness and even misery are waiting for us there, too. Maybe after a brief sense of satisfaction, we quickly realize that unfulfilled-ness has followed us and still exists on the inside. Not that you can't have enormous success and material comforts and be happy, as we will explore, you just have to get your priorities straight. You have to allow your soul to be part of the process.

Super rich, super outwardly seemingly successful people can actually be the most miserable, as they look around at everything they have accomplished and acquired and still feel unsatisfied at a deep level. Actor Jim Carrey famously stated this concept on point in a commencement speech, saying, "I think everybody should get rich and famous and do everything they ever dreamed of so they can see that it's not the answer."

So what is the answer? And *WHEN* is it time to stop seeking outside solutions for our inside problems? When can we actually live in a space that represents the qualities of life that are important to us? *WHEN* will we be expressing creativity, having those meaningful conversations, and not be preoccupied, but actually available for those we love, INCLUDING ourselves? *WHEN* is the right time to delve deeper into your spiritual journey?

The good news, I've realized, is that there doesn't necessarily need to be a designated, set-aside time when that never-ending day-to-day list of things to do is complete to step on the path of personal evolution and spiritual growth. WE ARE ALREADY ON OUR SPIRITUAL PATH. Whether acknowledging it or not, evolution is already taking place.

The opportunities to evolve, or subconscious tactics of blocking that evolution are ever present. Even if you say, *I do not have a spiritual practice, I am not on a spiritual journey,* indeed, as time passes, that lack of a decision and non-action toward growth has spiritual implications. Implications in the ways you do not connect with those around you, in the meaningful words left unsaid because you were not in a space of being conscious. Your lack of being proactive on your spiritual path will undoubtedly leave the higher self in you unrealized, certainly leaving a void inside of you and a void in the lives with whom you are a part. On any given day, if you are willing to see it, in almost any given moment, the chance for growth, expansion and finding zen are happening. Life itself is an evolutionary journey of the soul. You are evolving. It's happening now, today, even in this moment.

We could travel the globe, taking in all the wonders of the world, seeking as we wander, in search of some soul-shaking, life-altering truth, but we don't have to. Lessons and blessings are ubiquitous in the people and circumstances of our everyday lives. Lessons and blessings are present in the seemingly smallest things, and even in the seemingly most annoying people we encounter. In your ordinary life, the Universe is offering you challenges, opportunities, insights, solutions and truth every single day. Even without climbing to a mountaintop or holding a single yoga pose, the answers we seek are available not just to the Monks and the Spiritual teachers of the world, but to You and to Me.

If the life you are living or the way you are living is not satisfying or does not feel good significantly more often than it feels bad, there are other possibilities for you. With some effort and some tweaks in your internal landscape, you will find even if your external circumstances do not change, YOU will. I can promise if you engage on your path of spiritual growth, inserting more awareness and a clearer intention into your day to day, you will experience more of the spiritual qualities you long for: peace, love, hope, joy, meaning and connection. Not because you do it my way, but because you find YOUR way.

You do not have to be broken or suffering to benefit from consciously engaging on your path of spiritual growth. Maybe you are suffering. Maybe you are suffering a lot—toward your breaking point. Or maybe you're like I was, suffering a little with an internal angst in quiet moments wanting more contentment and meaning. Or perhaps you are just wanting clarity and confidence that you are on the right path expanding toward your potential and making the most of your time on earth.

Sometimes the death of a loved one or loss or other monumental occurrence smacks you in the face with the fragility of this life. Such events and trials can ignite a desire, making you more hungry than ever to make the days, the moments and the full picture of your lifetime purposeful. It suddenly becomes imperative to seek the connection, love and joy your heart desires. None of us wants to be the person, poet, and philosopher Henry David Thoreau so eloquently spoke of who leaves this earth with "the song of our hearts left unsung!" Whatever the catalyst, I believe each of us gets to a place where we question our purpose and if the road we are on is going to enable us to get there. If we want to discover and proceed on our path of growth with less stumbling—less running into the same walls again and again—we need to understand the journey and we will need some tools to help us navigate it.

CHAPTER 3

The Journey: And So It Begins

"Find yourself and lose your misery."

—M. ARNOLD

*W*ith your decision to seek a better way, in realizing that outside circumstances, outside accolades, material possessions and ego-driven "likes" on social media have NOT made you happy, you begin the process of awakening. This awakening is the first step on your journey of growth. You begin to realize this truth: there are not enough external experiences, possessions or affirming pats on the back by others that will ever fill your heart and soul with the lasting peace you desire.

For sure by *now*—at this stage of life—you thought you would feel different. You thought you would feel *better*. You know you want more. You acknowledge that something needs to change and you acknowledge that change is not happening. With this awareness, you can now get real about how much you are or are not being proactive in the direction your life is going. How much time, if any, have you been spending on things that will have the most impact on your future—your personal and spiritual growth?

A big part of feeling stuck and feeling unhappy at any given moment, is the belief that circumstances need to be different. People need to be different. *If only* things were different *then* you would be free to be happy and embrace your higher Self. *Then* you could find the peace you so desire.

If you are suffering, there is a shift that needs to be made. You've lost sight of your own power. Even the most minute change in your thoughts, beliefs, words, or actions can transmute some of the pain and lack of fulfillment you are experiencing and re-direct your focus. Small changes within yourself can yield surprisingly big results. Like scripture promises, "If ye have faith as a grain of mustard seed, ye shall say unto this mountain, remove hence to yonder place; and it shall remove; and nothing shall be impossible unto you." (Matthew 17:20) If that's not power, I don't know what is!

We say we have faith, and if you've read any other spiritual growth books, you've heard that things will *always work out in the end* or that there is Divine order. Part of us believes things will work out. But in between moments of having faith and moments of trying to convince ourself to have faith, is a whole myriad of non-faith thinking: anxiety, worry, stress, complaining, fretting and what if-ing. Part of you may desperately want to believe it's true that "everything is going to be OK." I can promise you if you get on a conscious path and do the spiritual work laid out ahead, you will live in the realization that in addition to hoping and believing that everything *will be* OK, you will come to KNOW that everything IS OK. All is well.

Some people make the association of a spiritual journey only in regard to their relationship with God or a Higher Power. The truths the Bible teaches thread themselves through each concept, no doubt. *Zen in High Heels* is not meant to replace or challenge your religious beliefs. It is recognizing that you can have your faith or religion but still be experiencing a messy, complicated, very unpeaceful life.

Look at this book as a supplemental resource. While I believe God breathes breath in all things spiritual and is there every step along the way as a steadfast companion if you allow him to be; to fix your life, your spiritual journey in the context of these chapters is primarily about coming to terms with your relationship with YOU. This expanded part of your spiritual journey becomes recognizing the proximity of where you are in life and how in alignment you are living with WHO you really are and what you are called to be doing.

At a fundamental level, all qualities of zen require You being right with You.

If you operate with your spirituality only being acknowledged at church or at a funeral, or even just in yoga class, and you keep your family relationships, your professional work, your physical health, or any other parts of your life in a separate compartment, you will undoubtedly experience dissonance and discord. When it comes down to it, to experience peace, we must harmonize our lives inside and out. Walking in the world and letting your spiritual conscious-ness influence all areas of your life in big and in small ways is where the magic lies. This is what we are seeking. As the saying goes, *We are not merely human beings having a spiritual experience, rather we are spiritual beings having a human experience.*

It is in embracing our life journey in this way, as an opportunity for spiritual discovery in all areas of our life, at all times, that we can purposely begin to pay attention and participate. Less wandering aimlessly, wondering if we are doing what we should be doing, less drama, less self-doubt, less need to hide or to judge or to fix things. These "needs" for the most part, drop away. Our life begins to unfold in the way it is meant to—in a way that we can show up and be present for it. Satisfaction, fulfillment, and zen begin to appear.

Spiritual work encompasses ALL areas of life. The work that is calling for your attention can manifest in any part of your human experi-ence: physical symptoms, emotional stress, limited sport or career performance, financial hardship, relationship difficulties, and the list goes on. If you believe any part of your life needs to be different in this moment for you to experience inner peace, there is work to be done!

Spiritual perspective on everyday experiences makes it much easier to not get caught up in what usually turn out to be the petty details in life that seem to drag us down, suck our energy and veer us off track. Spiritual perspective instills hope that there is, indeed, Divine order, in which case all IS well. I can worry less and release part of the proverbial weight of the world on my shoulders back to the Universe for proper tending to.

In *Zen in High Heels* I am acknowledging the spiritual journey as a reconciliation process. Your spiritual journey seeks to reconcile the physical You: the You that is moving about and expressing yourself in the world, with the internal You: your soul, the deeper part of you that is infinite, eternal, and holds your deepest desires and all of your potential. The internal You holds your truth. This is where you find your way. You will find what you need to live happy and fulfilled, with purpose and meaning.

There are countless people who have a Bible or some spiritually inspired book by their bedside. People who, on a daily basis, enjoy a page or chapter that somehow resonates with their soul as true. The problem is, you get out of bed, go into the world, or answer the phone call and BAM! Your emotions and "reality" hit you right between the eyes. The peace and truth you just read about are nowhere in sight!

Ughh. Why? How is it that we would like to have faith in what is promised, but still struggle with the seemingly endless conflicts and situations that hijack our lives and hold hostage our zen, despite our very best intentions?

You can decide to read extra pages of that inspirational book the next night, but *still* experience no tangible difference in your day-to-day life. Despite your desire to act and feel more "spiritual," you still find yourself annoyed, frustrated, bummed out, overwhelmed, or whatever it is that you experience *other than zen*! This is because in addition to fueling yourself with spiritual teachings, you must take ACTION. You must not only trust the truths you have read or heard, but you must also dig within yourself to find the gaps. Identify the gaps between the concepts of truth you long to experience in your life, and your current reality.

Let's be honest, it is easy to hear teachings of spiritual principles and feel inspired. It is quite another thing to figure out HOW the HELL to apply those concepts to your actual life! Turns out the advice is not really as daunting as it sometimes seems, but equally not always clear as to how to actually execute it, for example, with your mother-in-law or that annoying co-worker.

Again, You must identify the gaps between what you believe or hope to be true and how your life is actually unfolding. Acknowledge the places in your life where you are experiencing less than desirable results. You must incorporate self discovery into your life!

It only makes sense that as we become more aware of the gaps and more consciously engaged in the process of addressing those gaps that our path will become illuminated. The spiritual principles laid out ahead will give you the understanding you need to bridge those gaps and the illumination to see what next steps need to be taken along your way. You will gain clarity. Only then are we able to grow in ways the darkness did not allow. We are then able to participate more consciously in propelling our lives in the direction of our truest desires. You will wake up to the blocks and limitations that up until this point you just accepted as reality, or as necessary parts of life. You will learn the truth of what you can and cannot control. This understanding will give you a new sense of confidence about your life. Zen will follow.

As your internal confidence grows, you will rely less and less on the opinions of and on the approval of others to believe you are OK. A very welcome realization that you can make your own choices, find your own way, and build your own self confidence. Thus cutting one of the cords that may have been keeping you captive from experiencing your zen—the need for the approval of others.

Along my way, I had to discover not only what principles resonated as true for me but also what would stick when applied. I needed to understand how to incorporate the teachings and use them as actual tools to fix or improve challenges I faced in my day-to-day life. I needed to understand spiritual principles in a way that would propel me forward in my growth. Yes, my heart and soul want to know the truth, but equally I want to experience truth! I want answers and RESULTS for my life!

In the midst of whatever drama or trauma you may be experiencing, or in the drudgery of what your everyday life feels like, it may seem like you are merely a passenger on the ship of your life, not realizing the steering wheel is within reach! So much of your life experience feels out of your control, yet there is enormous untapped power just waiting for you to claim it. By engaging in your spiritual work laid out ahead, you will cultivate an awareness that allows you to understand this.

I want you to have the realization that any cycle of frustration and misunderstandings and resulting turmoil you may be experiencing does not have to continue! Somewhere deep inside you know this—but how can you access the answers you need for yourself? HOW do we actually break unhealthy cycles and patterns and those oh-so limiting beliefs?

It's like a perfect recipe. We want to get the ingredients just right, based on our past, our current experience, and where we see our future. When each of us takes the time to heal our past, to learn to live in the reality of our present, and to consciously expand our horizons of what the future might look like, we will be led to where truth lies: this is where YOU will find YOUR truth and all of the answers that you seek. Healed past suffering and less suffering TODAY will be beautiful rewards of your effort.

As you will see, *Zen in High Heels* aka personal evolution toward your potential starting right here and right now, is not something that just strikes like lightning, it is a process. It is a process that is always accepting of starting you from exactly where you are. If you are feeling that nudge or longing for more meaning and inner peace, as I was, do not think you have to wait for things to slow down, circumstances to change, or get your ducks in a row before you can begin your journey. It starts with awareness: which is available anywhere, at any time! The only prerequisites are that you are breathing and that your mind and heart are open.

Pursuing spiritual growth is not about perfection. It is about progress. It is about potential. We just need to understand where our discontent originates and we need tools to be able to turn any struggle into a platform from which we are able to learn, grow, and jump off as a better version of ourselves. A truer version of ourselves.

Many parts of the process appear as challenges, but when you seek truth for yourself with an open heart, the rewards of growth are exponential and interestingly, challenges become reframed as chances for growth, even gateways to freedom! Freedom from the entanglement of unhealthy, unserving patterns of thinking and behavior that have bound you in the past.

The life I am living should be a manifestation of my soul's desires. My life should reflect who I am at the deepest level. My life should feel nourishing to my soul. We are all meant to experience life in a way that involves creativity, authentic self-expression, deeper connections with others and love: lots of love. We are meant to remember our way back to the understanding that we are much more the same than we are different and that we are all connected. We are meant to come back to a place where love is revealed in all areas of our lives.

Wow, what a concept! Can you imagine love being revealed in all areas of your life? It's worth striving for. Our soul originates in this world, and leaves this world to return to its purest state: the state of absolute LOVE. If love is our true nature, and love is what we long for most, how does this quest to experience it become so complicated? How is it we find ourselves in pain and suffering and what feel like very UNloving circumstances so often along the way? Why does love feel elusive in many of our day-to-day experiences and with many of the people with whom we encounter?

I believe our capacity for love is infinite and when we start breaking through some of the walls that the mind and society try to contain us within, we begin seeing results: finding love where we did not believe love existed. Find the invisible walls in your life and be willing to challenge them. There is no describing the strength, personal power, and growth you feel when those boundaries are moved...even an inch out of your way. Finding love equals finding transformation.

Being loving sounds so simple and at the same time, almost impossible. Expressing love doesn't seem that feasible when we experience real life dilemmas in the "real" world in which we are living. If you find yourself thinking, *I've got some messy, complicated shit going on in my life, and LOVE is not a practical solution!* What I am saying is that love is, in fact, your true nature, and as you do the spiritual work, operating from a place of your truth (which is love) will result in affecting all of the relationships and situations you find yourself in. Of this I am certain: your spiritual journey toward enlightenment always unveils the presence of love, even in places you did not believe love existed. Enlightenment shows you love where you could not see it before.

Finding glimpses of love in situations or people that would ordinarily have taken you down a dark or negative road, are moments of realizing the work you are doing is indeed having a real impact on your life! This is one of the many rewards of your spiritual work. You realize that zen—love, peace and fulfillment—can occur spontaneously in very unexpected moments and very unexpected places.

I have experienced such moments. Moments in the past that would have caused such turmoil. Then one day, as a welcome side effect of my work, the same person and the same circumstance presented themselves but things were different. I was different. I could walk away with peace and a heart practically bursting with gratitude! So grateful for my new perspective. Grateful for the zen I experienced as a result of my newfound understanding of my role, understanding my sphere of influence, and my ability to choose new, better responses based on that understanding!

I can honestly say when I find myself in the midst of unhappy or undesirable circumstances, I can also almost always say simultaneously that I feel peace in my soul. At the very same time: undesirable circumstances going on outside of me, but peace on the inside of me. Maybe this is the kind of peace the Bible promises in Philippians 4:7: "peace that passes all understanding." When I stepped on my path of exploration to find my zen, I hoped it would be possible to find that inner peace more often. I have now come to understand that peace is *always* available—just waiting to be claimed! When this starts to happen for you, you will be in awe and amazement.

On your quest to go deeper and pull the longing of your soul forward, your willingness to be 100% honest with yourself—perhaps for the first time ever—and see the truth you have lived up until now will undoubtedly, at times, feel painful, disappointing, and even overwhelming. But this fragile time is also hope-filled. Meaning getting from where you realize you are to where you deeply want to be can feel hopeless at the level of your mind, but at the spiritual level, there is nothing BUT HOPE. Hope remains. Hope is intrinsically attached to all possibility. As you work to find and explore previously unseen possibilities, your hope will reemerge. You will have so much hope for the changes and improvements on the horizon awaiting you!

It is my desire that the tools and principles that proved to be invaluable along my way will help you too. However, I am in no way trying to convince you to do what I do or believe what I believe. I do not claim to have a golden ticket to *your* zen—which may or may not include high heels! However, I am certain that being more intentional with your spiritual work will lead you to the clarity, peace, and meaning you seek. As you learn to come into communion with your soul more often, your path will be revealed: a path of light and love.

I've been alluding to this premise: ALL aspects of your journey of spiritual growth begin and end with Y-O-U. Let's continue and learn how this is so.

PART II

Building Your Foundation

CHAPTER 4

"We have met the enemy, and he is us."

—JOHN F. KENNEDY

Enemy #1 for blocking spiritual growth and keeping you from experiencing an abundance of zen in your life, is *you*. More specifically, YOUR MIND, which can be a helpful tool for you, or a torturer. Personal growth always begins here, in the privacy of your own mind. Our private thoughts hold tremendous power in moving us toward an expanded version of ourselves or keeping us confined in the construct of the way things have always been. The mind is an astounding force and, at the same time, incredibly underutilized for the purpose of personal growth. At any moment, your mind can either conceal or reveal the innermost parts of your own heart where your zen resides.

Consider the following statements; perhaps you can relate:

I AM STRONG. Well, I'm pretty strong. I'm strong sometimes. Strong at work but not so strong when it comes to standing up to my domineering parent. I'm strong with my husband, but not so strong when wanting to decline the P.T.A. position.

I AM AT PEACE. Well, I would be if so-and-so would stop doing such-and-such, which really stresses me out! And I do have some anxiety about how this other thing I'm dealing with will turn out. And after all the suffering I saw on the news, how can I possibly feel total peace?

MATERIAL THINGS DON'T REALLY MAKE PEOPLE HAPPY. Well, yes, of course, except if only I could afford a new Hermes bag—I would surely exude happiness as I walk around with it, and people could see how stylish and successful I am. And, I'll be honest, my neighbor must be happier than I am because she drives a brand new BMW. I'm certain if I had a newer car, I would be happier.

I AM WORTHY OF LOVE. Well, as long as I don't ruffle any feathers by speaking up about my true feelings, as long as nobody sees the secrets I hide about myself, and as long as I keep the weight off.

Can you hear the struggle? Even from these few simple examples: the conflict of wanting to embrace spiritual teachings, declaring them true, but in my mind having an inner dialogue that is different. Part of me does believe them to be true, believes in the promise they hold, even for ME. But then there's "reality," or what I am experiencing as my reality, which seems in conflict.

Who exactly is it we are in conflict with? Who is inside of you debating what you want to believe and what you actually do believe? How do we put an end to the internal struggle and make these spiritual truths, all spiritual truths, real for us? Is it continued practice? Saying it until we believe it? If we say it for years, will it finally embed in our consciousness, take root and grow? Should we fake it 'til we make it? Would posting it on sticky notes throughout my house make it so? Do we need to reach a certain age of maturity before it "clicks?" Here's your retirement check, and it comes with a magic eraser to rid your mind of unwanted thoughts and beliefs! NOW, *finally*, you can say you have unbreakable inner strength, you are at peace, you do not need material things to make you happy, and you are worthy of being loved! Is that when we finally believe it, feel it and live it?

So here we are, back at the familiar place of having a vague comprehension of something we want to experience: these declarations of truth, but not understanding how to incorporate them and make them real in our actual life. Where do we begin? How do we begin to get our mind in alignment with our new goal of enlightenment? As previously mentioned, acknowledging dissatisfaction with some or all aspects of your life begins activating the realization that something needs to change. This process of awareness takes place in the mind.

You may have been surprised when I declared YOU as enemy number one! It may sound negative or disheartening to say the root of your unhappiness and lack of zen lies inside of YOU. But you will find this truth is actually empowering. It is great news that once you dig deep, look at what's there, acknowledge and heal any wounding, past suffering, and perceived limitations, and see what is needing to be expressed that you can then live from your place of truth and authenticity. *Regardless* of anyone else's past, present, or future words or behavior toward you, you will realize who you are and how you want to move in life. Now THAT is empowering!

David Goggins, former Navy SEAL and author of *Can't Hurt Me,* refers to our conflicting and negative thoughts as an "enemy" that lives inside us, corroborating JFK's statement that the biggest adversary we are up against for evolution and growth is not some outside evil force, but rather an ever-present and deeply entrenched part of our own mind. According to Goggins, this *enemy* that exists within ourselves would much rather you stay lazy and comfortable than grow and be excellent. He says this *enemy*, this deeper unconscious part of our mind, will ALWAYS have the "tactical advantage" directing your choices and behavior, as it has been with you from the beginning and knows all of your deepest secrets, your fears and your insecurities. So we must work harder than we even realize to get around the sneaky, sneaky ways of our mind.

When we acknowledge the possibility that there is perhaps an enemy inside our own mind and start the process of noticing our thoughts, we usually realize this power center that's been driving our behavior is a little unpredictable and unruly. Or maybe the opposite is true at times: too rigid or too closed off from allowing you to see another way than the way you are going, let alone illuminating the actual endless possibilities that exist for you.

When we start to pay attention, it is pretty undeniable that we have been operating with what Buddhists refer to as a monkey mind! Our thoughts, like monkeys, are jumping here, jumping there, running in circles, easily distracted, and haphazardly giving our attention to random things! Oftentimes this internal dialogue of thought is relaying shitty, sabotaging messages with some kind of authority as if it speaks the truth. The first step in achieving your zen begins with noticing the thoughts in your mind.

If you're like most people, you may not have really even considered the random thoughts going on in your mind. You probably were not aware that the never-ending dialogue is something to purposefully pay attention to, or, even more importantly, to challenge its source. We're just so used to that internal chatter as part of our everyday experience. The thoughts are happening, like a voice in our head. Observing, judging, blaming, maybe even hurling insults at yourself and others. It is this voice that creates insecurity or unworthiness. This voice creates the disparity between our truest human potential and our ability to actually experience that potential for ourselves, despite the fact that you are as capable of all good things and as worthy of all good things as anyone else walking the planet.

Enlightenment teachers seem to agree that the majority of the thoughts we are having are not actually truly us. Did you catch that

ZEN IN HIGH HEELS

distinction? They are *your* thoughts, inside *your* head, but they are not really you. Whoa, what? Most thoughts are just a chatty representative of one aspect of your identity. The part of your identity meant to analyze and interpret your emotional environment and your actual environment to keep you safe, or what it considers to be safe.

Michael A. Singer, in his book, *Untethered Soul,* goes so far as to refer to this part of our mind as a live-in "roommate." It's as if another separate entity lives with us, inside our head. Singer made me laugh with his realization that this mental "roommate" would not shut up! Even babbling away in the shower! LOL.

Psychology and spiritual teachings refer to this part of our psyche as the EGO. The ego is the part of our mind designed to mediate between the conscious and unconscious world. Striving always to protect us from real or perceived-as-real threats to its existence. The ego develops a big part of its frame of reference in our childhood. That's why as an adult, if you go to counseling for a problem, they will most often want to talk to you about your childhood. Many of the entanglements of the mind, from which we have to untangle to find peace, originated in childhood.

Based on your past experiences, the ego has a perception as to what is a threat and what is necessary to keep you safe. But as we will discover, the ego works hard to keep you in a box with the lid sealed tight. Like a helicopter parent, looking over your shoulder at all times to make sure you do not make what it perceives as a "wrong" or "dangerous" move! Even if, in actuality, there is no threat, this part

Your actual truth is waiting to be discovered—like the treasure mentioned earlier—there in the silent space of your meditation. Your truth is the most valuable treasure you can acquire in your life-time. No other treasure compares.

With a meditation practice, you will be able to discern which ideas are yours and which ideas are not yours. Is this what you want, or actually what your parents want? Is this what you want to do, or are you doing it because it is what your neighbors are doing? Will this product or service make your life better, or is this what marketers want you to believe?

Meditation serves as an introduction opportunity to the deeper parts of your Self. Get quiet so that each day you can meet with that deep inner part of you. Your own personal meet and greet: *Hey Girl*!

Greet the You that is your private, deeper thoughts and feelings. Spend some time alone with Her. What does she want to say? What does she want to do? What's bothering her? As time passes, your meditation becomes a sacred space of communion between your physical self and your soul's voice. A time to check in, listen, hear, restore, and reboot back to You after you have been bombarded by all the noise of life.

Meditation gives us revelations of *who* we really are; it provides the space we need to be honest with ourselves. All spiritual growth occurs from a place of truth and honesty. As you come to know your truth, you are able to reflect on and respect where you have been, where you are now, and what you aspire for yourself moving forward.

It is shocking when we first decide to still our mind by cutting the noise. So much noise! Forget the voice in your head for a moment, start with the cell phone, the television, the internet, the radio in the car, social media, conversations, and opinions of friends and family you interact with. We are addicted to being mentally overstimulated, which serves the part of us that is resistant to change. No time it seems, to deal with how we really feel, to tend to what we really need, or address what is really going on.

Awareness will result in you paying attention to your life in a more purposeful way. In paying attention, you will probably be shocked by all of the distractions. The outside world is always tantalizing you to think a certain way, look a certain way, and spend your money a certain way.

Cut the mental stimulation by cutting the noise. Get peace and quiet whenever you can find it. Really, anytime you have the opportunity to shush the outside influences of noise, take it! This could mean turning off the radio in the car, staying off your phone on the bus or carpool, muting the commercials while watching TV, or breaking the habit of putting on the news first thing in the morning. No inner-peace seeker has declared that twenty-four hour world news feed was part of their path to enlightenment. Said no one, ever.

Get used to using more discretion about what goes into your brain and consciousness. We all know the thought process: if you feed a child a bunch of sugar, he will go wild, act crazy, and be unable to sit still and concentrate! The mind acts similarly to surface-level visual and audio stimuli—it gets hyped up, overstimulated, and has difficulty focusing! Be vigilant of the nonstop stimulation. Give your brain some peace and quiet.

It takes courage to sit still. It is definitely a conscious decision in today's world! Acknowledge the need to make adjustments. Be honest with yourself about the ways you remain distracted. And how you justify it. Anything distressing or disturbing gets shoved to the back burner while we check our phone, volunteer for one more needy cause, and binge-watch six hours of must-see TV. Settling your mind by quieting your environment whenever you can is an essential step on your path to zen.

Whenever possible, I meditate lying down, eyes closed, with an intention of tuning out and tuning in. Tuning out the noise of the world, the opinions of others, and the day-to-day distractions that take away from my priorities. Tuning in to Me, my heart, the most quiet space where zen resides. It's like taking an empty bucket to the well and filling it up with zen...which you can then carry back to the next experience your day brings. You can bring that zen to your next interaction with the outside world. All age-old and newer versions of spiritual attunement call for some form of meditation. Quiet time. As far back as the Bible. God instructs us: "Be still and know." (Psalm 46:10)

If your first few meditation attempts evoke discomfort or negativity in your mind, hang in there. Do a tiny bit at a time. If your first day, week, or month of meditation do not reveal even a single meaningful peep from your deeper self, do not be discouraged! You may even feel a sense of increased stress as your mind runs through all of the other things you should be doing. It's OK. Give it time. The neural pathways of your brain are used to firing on what is right in front of you. It may take time to strengthen the ones that run deeper. The deeper pathways that connect your brain to your heart.* (*DISCLAIMER: I do not know the exact science, but you get my attempt to illustrate the point!)

Acknowledge any uncomfortable feelings by actually thinking or even whispering an inner dialogue that you are interested in going deep. Acknowledge the resistance that you are feeling. Promise that deeper part of you that you are in a safe environment. Let her know you are open and interested in getting beyond the noise to just BE with her and listen. *I want to know who you are. I want to know what you need from me.* Then be still, and listen. It might feel a little weird or hokey at first, but you are laying the groundwork for new neural pathways that will ultimately connect you with the truth you are seeking: your truth! Your beautiful, honest, sacred truth awaits!

If I have a particularly daunting thing going on in my life, and holding still and being quiet only seems to give the monkeys in my mind permission to swing in circles with that issue that's troubling me, I will revert to my headphones and a guided meditation. Because let's be honest, sometimes being alone with your thoughts is not a very nice space to be in! Enlightenment seems nowhere to be found there!

There are countless guided meditations available via the internet, YouTube, apps, and other digital downloads to get you started. Search for one in which you feel soothed by the voice and relaxed and drawn in by the content. Perhaps one with no words, only music that is specifically recorded to relax your mind and body and will help you get started. Be willing to try different ones. YouTube can be an amazing meditation partner. You can get as specific with your search as you want. For example, "meditation to gain confidence" or "meditation to heal the body." Don't give up if the first or second meditation you listen to is not for you; there are THOUSANDS.

I get it, nothing makes you feel more like a zen failure than making the effort to meditate, but finding yourself totally annoyed by the pace, the tone or the visuals offered by the wrong guided meditator for you.

Resistance will tell you, *This is not working! This sitting still stuff is not for me!* Be persistent, and you will find one or more guided meditations that are a fit for you and can help you escape your overactive mind and find just the right amount of restoration to get you through the rest of your day refreshed. It's not uncommon these days to find an actual meditation class you can attend in your church or community. Alone or with the support of guidance, quiet time is the first step on the path of a more enlightened version of You!

Meditation Level One: mindfulness. May be done anywhere at any time, even in an activity. Cut the noise. Like a dietary cleanse—cut the crap out! So much crap vying for your attention. Quieting the outside world in and of itself has healthy benefits. This level can be achieved for example in yoga, running, gardening, even housekeeping. Mindfulness can be practiced by paying attention. Notice your breath, notice your surroundings, the way your body feels. Use your senses, be aware.

Meditation Level Two: tuning in. This is where the truth lies. Practice Level One for a while, then surrender deeper in your practice to Level Two. IF THERE IS AN END GOAL OF MEDITATION, IT IS TO LIVE IN ALIGNMENT WITH YOUR TRUTH. With this alignment, the drama in your mind and in your life drops away because you no longer thrive on it or create it. Your actions and words become in alignment with your values that have now become clear to you—therein lies peace for you. The peace of mind and peace of spirit we are all seeking has a chance to be revealed.

When you learn to honor what is brought to consciousness in your meditation, you will find your thinking and your choices change. Not all at once. You may have heard someone tout how meditation changed their life. And no doubt it did, but it takes time. The changes you experience may be subtle at first. You may not gain all the peace and calm you desire in the first thirty days, but you may perhaps notice you feel less anxious. Progress, indeed! Your default reaction of quick temper may subside. Progress, indeed! Consistent practice will lead to consistent results, and you will find the answers you seek.

When you gain glimpses of your truth in meditation and let that guide you in the right direction, the path toward your enlightened life becomes illuminated. Those truths then become the compass. Even if only a little bit, you gain clarity for the next step. A consistent meditation practice will help you discern not only which thoughts originated from the desires and expectations of others, but also which thoughts are just your reactionary mind: preprogrammed, illusionary, fear-based ego mind. It is only from this soul-based perspective that you have awareness now of the dilemmas your mind has created for you. This awareness serves as a springboard for you to implement other tools and spiritual practices laid out in the next few chapters to manifest your potential and experience your zen.

The soul speaks softly and is found in quiet space, but as a warrior: unaffected by the *what ifs* and the *I don't think I can*. When you tap in and listen, the warrior aspect of the soul will fight for you and your truth like no one else has ever done! It is steely and abundant in what you need. Like the constitution of First Responders—always calm in turmoil and tragedy, but has answers to deal with the situation at hand.

As you become a more conscious version of yourself, you will still experience pain in painful situations. But from a perspective of more awareness, you will be able to neutralize the experience and get through the negative emotions without the drama or destructive patterns of things like booze, drugs, or dragging others down with you. Growth through spiritual work even allows you to experience a painful situation with reverence. Reverence to being human and reverence to learning and to your process of evolution.

Don't get me wrong, meditation itself does not really SOLVE anything. Meditation reminds you of who you are, despite what is going on in your life or how stressed you might feel; in getting yourself centered and quieted down, you are reminded that you are OK. And meditation facilitates awareness to issues that need addressing outside of the meditation space. It's not that you meditate, and now you don't have problems. You meditate, and now you are better able to deal with the problems, or you are blessed with an awakening of what the real problems are, which may not be what your ego had you believing all along.

When you get into the process of seeking your truth in meditation, what you previously thought and accepted as "normal" or solid ground, you may now realize, is not. Challenging long-held beliefs can range from uncomfortable to actually painful or scary. You may wonder, *What if I cannot handle what is in there?* Either (A) because you are aware of some of the really painful shit you have been through and spent your whole life suppressing, or (B) because you have no idea what you will discover!

Here's the thing, the age or developmental place you were in when events or interactions of your past occurred was not an age or developmental phase that would allow you to process or healthily deal with the circumstance, event, confusion or trauma. That is why it is still there, in you. However, now you are different. Now you can look at it through the lens of the You who is older, the You who has more perspective. You can acknowledge and tend to the memory with the tenderness it requires and with compassion for yourself. Both for your younger Self who endured something, and your current Self who has been doing the best she can. We will look closer at healing such deep wounding again later, but we are acknowledging here that many times the initial realization that something indeed is waiting for our attention takes place during your meditation time. Now that we are no longer allowing our mind to run wild 24/7, we are able to tend to issues within ourselves that need tending to.

This is the foundation of your spiritual work as an adult: to heal what needs healing. Emotional healing allows you to live today and tomorrow as who you really are: an uninhibited being of light and love. And THIS way of living not only yields rewards for you and your experiences moving forward, it also serves to impact everyone else you interact with in the most profound ways.

You getting clarity about You in meditation increases your chances for that real connection with others that you so long for. You will find peace, vulnerability, and real connection are just around the corner, ready for your arrival because with the awareness meditation brings, you open the door to express yourself more fully and others can respond to that truer version of you. As you steadfastly dig and keep doing your spiritual work, you are truly strengthening future generations! You will benefit, your kids will benefit, their kids will benefit, and the legacy continues.

You can be the one to break the cycle of known or unknown limitations and sabotaging patterns in your family. Resolving deep-rooted issues will alleviate any belief of "lack" in your mindset that the unhealed wounds may have instilled in you. The lies the subconscious mind will communicate with you TODAY regarding any past unhealed wounds, no matter how big or how small the wounds are, will always portray you in a way that is diminished and limited. *You are not worth whatever it is you desire. You do not have the support, the knowledge, or the strength to get through what has happened to you. You did not have the parents that "happy" people had.*

This is where therapy, or energy work, or some kind of support from the outside can help you assimilate issues that present themselves to you for a closer look. The uncovering of long-held deep issues you've been holding can disrupt your emotions or even your physical body. It is wise, not weak, to reach out for assistance from someone who is trained to support this process of growth and healing. Finding a professional to assist you in processing and working through the deeper issues that are now ready to be healed is invaluable.

Just remember: outside support is a tool, not a crutch. Another person does not hold the answers for you but can certainly help steady you and nourish you along your way. A good therapist can rearticulate your words, experiences and pains in a revised way. In a way without your filter of emotion or memory. This allows you to see better—more clearly—perhaps differently, allowing you to let go of it. Release it in its inhibitory form, giving you an "aha" moment, and freeing up the energy that was stuck, holding the trauma or dilemma there unhealed.

It really is possible to get through any pain, neglect and limitations placed on you by others once and for all. Whatever happened to you no doubt contributed to part of your way of navigating life, and can be attributed to what you've been using as coping mechanisms. But also, no doubt the pain you have experienced made you stronger in ways you would not have been otherwise. As real and as seemingly debilitating as painful experiences are, there is no obligation, spiritually or otherwise, that you must continue to hide or carry the heavy burden of them forward with you. Tend to the pain, get the help you need, and then allow yourself permission to be free.

If you are feeling some fear at this point, my advice is *NOT* to *not* be afraid. Fear is the ego trying to protect you. Feel the fear, but do the work anyway! Know that for a period of time, it may suck; the process of healing may require you to feel the hurt. Always remember that THE TRUTH WILL SET YOU FREE! It just takes time. You actually are free, but you do not fly overnight. It is a process of growing and testing your wings.

You will experience some peace while in meditation, but the real gift then becomes the peace you create in your life outside of meditation. The peace you create in your life with the newfound clarity your truth-seeking meditation practice gives you. If you would rate the noise in your head and stress level in your life a solid 9 on a scale of 1–10, meditation initially might get you to a 7 or 8. You will probably still have lots of chaos in your mind or in your life outside the meditation space. It is important to honor the process, and the progress. I believe this is where some people get frustrated or give up. There is an expectation, or a timeline. *Two steps of meditation = peace. Thirty days of meditation = zen.*

If I gave you a seed to grow corn, you would not plant the seed and come back tomorrow or even in two weeks and give up on it, or be sorely disappointed that it had not yielded a single ear of corn for you to eat! You would not say to me, "You promised this little seed would grow me corn, but look, it did not work!" You would more likely respect the process and the progress as the seed grows into its potential, ultimately enjoying the harvest that each step along the way allowed the seed eventually to become.

So as your life outside of meditation begins to calm down, respect each phase. You may get stuck somewhere along the way, say at stress level number 5. Don't judge it. You have nothing to lose by continuing with your meditation practice. But if you give up at any point, the potential of the harvest will undoubtedly remain unrealized and unclaimed by you. Be patient. Be gentle with yourself. You have your whole lifetime to continue to grow and evolve. Enjoy each step of the sure-to-be fascinating process, but do keep forging ahead!

Getting a grip on your thoughts and becoming acquainted with your potential requires practice. Old patterns will still weasel their way into your thinking and decisions. But as you practice words and actions more in alignment with your soul, you will begin to see progress. And noticing your own growth will be the assurance you need that you are on the right path. This is so very satisfying. You become backed by a personal power you never had before. Internal clutter and conflict dissipate, and you feel more aligned with the Universe.

As I mentioned, in raising your awareness through meditation, problems do not necessarily disappear. Your relationship with the problems changes. And you see more options for resolution in the same mess.

As a practical example: imagine someone spills red wine on your white sofa. All internal alarms fire in your mind! You FREAK OUT!! You are furious at the person for spilling the wine! You are mad at yourself for letting them drink red wine while sitting on your sofa. You try to navigate and monitor your outward re-action. You don't want to scream like a maniac (or maybe you do?). You know it was an accident, and accidents happen. You frantically wonder how to clean it up, if it will clean up, and/or how much it will cost to have it professionally cleaned or replaced.

Now what if you become aware of and purchase a new product that instantly cleans red wine spills? Can you imagine how your internal dialogue will change given the same circumstance? How much calmer, less reactionary, and judgmental you will need to be when the red wine spills on the white sofa? The red wine may still spill, but you are able to react differently. You can remain calm because your aware-ness has increased to include a possible solution. THAT is a basic example of what meditation results are like. You go back next time to a problem or something annoying, someone else messing up your situation, but you have access to a new solvent. A solvent to solve it. The situation still requires action, but you've got new tools. You don't lose your head over it. All is well. Or will be well again shortly!

I know spilled wine on a sofa doesn't equate to growth on your soul's path...or does it? Life is made up of so many small, random, seemingly insignificant moments in the grand scheme of things. If meditation and spiritual work can positively affect your way of dealing with these moments and make you less REactive in instances like this—how much better will life feel? Less REactive plus less stress equals more zen. Does *every* mini disaster require you to lose your temper? Plus, the point is that when we can practice and digest these concepts in smaller day-to-day 21st century ways, it allows the possibility to carry this awareness to bigger situations, and more substantial problems.

As you progress in your practice, you may find that many messes will clean up more easily, maybe more swiftly, with less agony. If or when an even bigger mess appears, you will have confidence that you can handle it, and you will have experience on how to manage your way through it. If you are deliberate about cleaning up each mess systematically—one layer at a time with an open mind as to what each piece means for you—you will find some improvement in your perspective at the bottom of that mess. Then it's on to the next one.

Meditation and spiritual work give you new tools, new solutions, and new ways of looking at things. You didn't realize your eyesight was 80/40 until you got the new pair of eyeglasses. Now you see 20/20!

Regular meditation is like getting corrective lenses for your perspective! 20/20 perspective or at least better than 80/40 spiritual vision is crucial for your zen!

You will find, your mind, if left unattended, will tend to dwell in the past and in the future, making it nearly impossible to ever live in THIS moment. But it is only in the *now* that you can find the joy you seek. Ruminating on the past can serve as a gateway for depression. Worrying about the future can serve as a gateway for anxiety. Peace is in THIS moment; it's nowhere else. When you can be present, it opens the door for ALL of the qualities of the life you seek. The sense of peace, love, groundedness, and connectedness are available when you find your way to THIS actual moment. If you have not been able to be present in the moment that is happening right here, right now, meditation is an invaluable first step. You will feel better when you take the time every day for this simple or sometimes not-so-simple practice of meditation.

Eckhart Tolle addresses the role the mind plays in keeping us in a state of struggle, worry, and anxiousness. In his book, *A New Earth*, Tolle teaches that you come to realize you can think a thought, but not BE the thought. You can feel an emotion, but not BE that emotion. I can feel angry, but that is not WHO I am. I am not an angry person, I am a peaceful person who is just feeling angry in this moment. A difference worth noting!

Becoming an observer of your thoughts leads to becoming an observer of your actions and, perhaps even more impactfully, an observer of your REactions. It is conscious awareness that allows just that extra moment of space in which to more purposefully respond and choose your next words and actions. And if you don't think such a space in response can change your life—well, just wait until you try it! So much of our struggle or drama, or suffering is actually in our interpretation or our REaction to what life brings us.

By being more aware, we become more responsible for our words and actions. We realize we have a choice and can choose not to react today the same way we did yesterday. That realization in and of itself allows for less anxiety and more calm moving forward. Knowing things can be different today than they were yesterday or different tomorrow than they are today offers up a big platter of HOPE! Hope that zen can be a reality, maybe even sooner than we believed possible.

It's so exciting to know we do not need to be held hostage to our feelings in every circumstance! There is power in choosing how we deal with or deny strong emotions when we experience them and, subsequently, how these choices affect our behavior. When we allow ourselves to seek to understand the value of and the root of our feelings, even the seemingly smallest circumstances become opportunities for growth.

It is only in this state of consciousness, brought about by our increased awareness, and supported by our meditation time that we can begin to choose differently. We realize now that we can change our behavior, and get our lives moving in the right direction. When we acknowledge the truth that we *always* have a choice, we unlock the vault holding for us enormous personal power! You really do not have to do things the way they have always been done. You really do not have to relate to the same people in the same way. Even what seem like small ingrained habits can be changed once you bring mindfulness to them, yielding actual *significant* change.

In my search for zen, I started to realize that I was making choices, big and small, conscious and unconscious, that substantially affected my ability to enjoy my life. We all need to be reminded of that now and then: that we ultimately are the ones making choices for ourselves and in those choices there is power. Power to change. Power to grow. Power to fuel ourselves in a different direction.

Turning the news on first thing in the morning is a choice. Having that third glass of wine on a weekday evening is a choice. Picking up the phone to gossip with someone about someone else is a choice. We will delve into all of this later, but understand that the first part of the process of growth is AWARENESS. With awareness you will realize many of the things we tolerate or accept as normal, are in fact, choices. You will come to understand your role and where and when you are actually contributing to your own unhappiness.

I have no doubt as your awareness increases, so will your opportunities to make choices toward growth and toward your potential. Reclaiming our power in the choices that we make allows us to be better today than we were yesterday. As Maya Angelou so famously said, "When you know better, you do better." Reclaim your freedom to do so—to do better TODAY!

In the beginning, you will make the right choices on some days and not on others. It's all part of the process. No judgment. It is meaningful to practice making different and better decisions for yourself in small ways and then grow toward bigger changes and choices. Don't set yourself up for failure with some predetermined idea of how quickly you should grasp this principle or how majorly your life should change.

An authentic journey of growth will present you with twists and turns that you cannot predict or expect. As you grow, you will identify new roads and paths to explore. It is a wonderful, unique, enchanting, and never-ending process!

It all starts with being proactive in this way—with awareness and choosing the better response more often than not—this is how our lives change for the better. It is in recognizing and seizing *choice* as ours in each moment. This is the kind of spiritual growth forward that is waiting for us at any moment. On most days we are presented with opportunities to interact differently. A plane trip around the world is not necessary for your spiritual growth, nor is fasting in a desert, or jumping through hoops of fire. There are daily chances right where you are to operate from a place of truth. Daily we get to choose love over fear and make decisions that contribute to our personal evolution and our zen.

An added bonus of regular meditation practice comes when you gain the awareness to recognize when a mess IS NOT YOURS! When you realize you are worrying or stressing about someone else or a situation you have ZERO control over, you can confidently leave it for its actual participants to deal with. Wow, what a revelation! Ahhhh—less drama for you! More peace for you! Newfound mental space for you to enjoy your zen in those high heels!

At this point in my growth, when a friend or family member confides in me about an undesirable circumstance they find themselves in, I actually feel excited for them! Empathetic, of course, for their pain, but excited for the possibility of breaking unserving patterns, and dealing with a truth that needs to be dealt with and the sunshine that is just over the horizon for them when they do! I pray for them. I pray that the pain or crisis will lead them to an empowered part of their path: an empowered version of themselves where they can find the strength and answers they seek held just beneath the level of consciousness they have been operating on up to this point.

I know they have to want to dig and do the work and find their way. I cannot do it for them. I used to struggle with this. But then I realized, *You cannot want more for someone than they want for themselves.* Period. Ever. Never works. Me engaging too deeply in "helping" them serves only to declare on some level that they cannot help themselves. And, me being immersed in someone else's drama—no matter how pure my intentions are—will begin to serve as a distraction from my own life and my own work, and my own personal things that need tending to. Stay tuned, this topic rears its head again!

Meditation will positively influence your life, no matter what. If you desire enlightenment, if you truly want to live at a higher level of consciousness, consistent quiet time alone will be part of the process. No exception. No book, or seminar, or retreat, or vision board will replace meditation. It is fundamental. Regular meditation is a non-negotiable part of achieving zen in high heels! Meditation is the foundation on which we will build the other practices. Let's continue.

CHAPTER 6

Gratefulness

"Some people grumble that roses have thorns; I am grateful that thorns have roses."

—ALPHONSE KARR

We have established that meditation is a core part of your routine on your path to zen. You will not manifest deep and sustainable change without a regular meditation practice. You are going to pay attention to your thoughts and eliminate unnecessary mental stimuli because you know that quiet time is going to make it possible to make a connection with the deeper, truer part of who you are. And, you may very well be seeking some outside support as you discover, process and heal parts of your Self or of your life experience that have been subconsciously holding you back. So, now what? Is that it? Does the zen show up, and you have never-ending bliss?

Meditation does serve as a power center for all of the principles moving forward in *Zen in High Heels*. If you meditate, will your life get better? Yes. If you meditate, will problems go away? No. However, you have taken the first steps and are being proactive in your personal evolution. You are no longer sleeping on autopilot, hoping things turn out well. You are no longer using outside noise and interactions with others to distract you from your path—or if you are, you are at least now becoming aware that you are!

As essential as meditation is and as transformative as meditation can be, you will want to build on that foundation with additional spiritual tools that will work together to stabilize you and reinforce a more authentic and more evolved way of being when you come out of your meditation space.

As all spiritual growth tools go, what I love so much about everything presented in *Zen in High Heels,* is that you do not need anybody else's participation or permission to use them! Spiritual tools are available at any time, and they don't cost a penny! It does not matter what someone else is doing, how old you are, or how much you weigh before these spiritual tools can work for you. Most importantly, they are *EFFECTIVE*! Integrating these principles will support your effort of operating in a higher state of consciousness. Increased zen will follow.

The next practice you are going to incorporate is: GRATITUDE. You are going to be grateful. You are going to look for things to be grateful for. You may respond, *Oh yes, of course, I am grateful. I'm grateful for my health. I'm grateful for my family.* Awesome. But I am talking about bringing more conscious awareness to everything you actually have to be grateful for on a daily basis. It's not merely a concept on the back burner, and when someone asks you, you have an obvious response. No, the way I suggest incorporating gratitude is that it needs to be part of your everyday awareness. It is this kind of gratitude practice that will serve as a building block for a strong, stable, zenful version of you as you grow forward on your path. To fuel your forward momentum on your path to enlightenment, make note (mentally or even better on paper) of five or more things you are grateful for every day. Start right now—put down this book, close your eyes and think of five things you are grateful for!

As much as I am certain you can think of something to be grateful for, in *Zen in High Heels* I am asking you to take it a step further. Take your gratitude a step further, enhanced by your new practice of meditation and the increased awareness you are bringing to your life now, and *feel* the gratitude in your heart. It's gratitude 2.0!

I can think I am grateful for the cake my aunt Mary made for my birthday. Then I can sit with that gratitude and feel it deeper. She actually took the time to buy the ingredients and to get out the pans and stir and mix and blend. She took the time to watch the timer on the oven, let the cake cool and then frost it for no other reason than to offer it to me as a symbol of love. Wow! That is something I can *be* grateful for, and also *feel* grateful for! It's synergistic. The thinking and the feeling then add another additional component. Now I'm having feelings of gratitude and appreciation for my aunt herself. So thankful to have her in my life! My gratitude has expanded!

Your gratitude can span from the biggest things: the healthy baby, or the promotion—to the smaller things: you got a front row parking space, your pet came to sit on your lap, or you found you had an extra tube of toothpaste as you unsuccessfully tried to squeeze any out of the one you were using! You scatter seeds of gratitude in that fertile soil of a mind that is aware and watch in amazement as they grow!

Gratitude is the duct tape in your personal growth toolbox! It can be beneficial in a multitude of scenarios. Sometimes, if only as a temporary solution for a pressing issue at hand. This "duct tape" (gratitude) can provide temporary relief, so the pipes don't burst so-to-speak.

Even when an entire day seems to have gone "wrong," nothing went as planned, I can end on a positive note. I can come back to center by spending a few minutes before I go to sleep thinking of at least ONE thing I can be thankful for that day. One thing that did go right, or that could have gone terribly worse. Even if I feel like I have to really dig for that one thing, 100% of the time, something always, eventually, comes to mind. It's funny because often, when I give my attention to that one thing and take a moment of thanks, I realize a couple of other things that went right. Now from *"This day sucked,"*

I can feel a slight lessening of the heaviness or burden I was feeling from the seemingly crappy day. There were redeeming qualities, I realize, and it is possible that tomorrow will be better.

As you know, gratitude did not magically change any of the sucky circumstances of the day I experienced; I am just in a less negative place about it. That's the basis of your spiritual progression. Life still happens, but you have healthy ways of shifting your attitude, which actually shifts your *experience* of the way things unfold. This profoundly affects your ability to hold on to your peace of mind. Your zen isn't waiting somewhere else for some other day; you can find it right here, right now, regardless of any circumstance.

As simple as it sounds, gratitude truly is a transformational practice. As we saw from that example of having a bad day, gratitude affects your perspective. It can lift your mood. This practice can instantly shift your focus from what you *do not* have to what you *do* have. From lack, to, if not abundance, at least awareness that you do have what is sufficient in this moment. Gratitude minimizes negativity and negates pessimism. Gratitude is the most simple way to get through a difficult moment. I'm talking about even *really* difficult moments.

In a big life crisis, gratitude can absolutely make the shift in you to make a meaningful difference. Let's use the example of my father dying at a relatively young age of 75. He was hospitalized not *with* COVID-19, but during COVID-19 so he was allowed no visitors for 39 days in the hospital! His trip to the ER began with foot pain. Although he didn't believe it would turn out to be anything too serious, the doctors discovered a blood clot. After days of tests and consideration of what his treatment should be, he unexpectedly had to endure a leg amputation. Something as serious and severe as a leg amputation all alone without any loved ones by his side for support! Blood pressure and other issues did not lend well to his ability to fully recover. He fought valiantly those last few weeks, but in the end his time on earth was over.

We did finally get to be with him when he was moved to hospice in the final 48 hours as he was dying. It was brutal, obviously not a positive life experience. Immediately following, and the days to come could, at times feel overwhelming with grief and emotional upset. I could not shake the very sad visions of seeing his beatdown body and spirit. As his mind was completely fine, his body was not going to hold on to life. There were so many things to be upset about! The state of the world: coronavirus keeping us apart— the hospital, despite his negative covid test and our negative covid tests still not letting us in to be by his side for OVER A MONTH! The thought of him being strong and brave enough to go through a leg amputation alone, making it through that, but not surviving anyway. There were a lot of legitimate reasons to feel bleak and cynical.

In the moments when I found myself feeling buried in it all, trying to make sense of it all, I had to pull out my spiritual tool of gratitude. Not to necessarily feel *good,* or even to feel *better*, but rather to negate the painful, dismal thoughts and feelings. I was obviously not grateful that my father had died. Obviously no gratitude in knowing I would never see or have a conversation with him again. I was not grateful for the circumstances around his passing.

So here is where the "practice" begins. I began searching and finding things in that moment of pain and grief that I could be grateful for. Finding gratitude in the fact that they did finally allow us at his bedside to be with him, he did not transition alone. Feeling grateful that I was physically and financially capable of jumping on the next flight out when I got the news that we may be allowed in to be with him. Grateful that I indeed did make it to see him before he passed. Grateful that he saw me, he knew I was there, and we were able to say *I love you* one final time. I had gratitude for the fact that I had him longer than some of my friends had their dads. Grateful he was no longer suffering. Which is true. The anguish he and we had already experienced was taking its toll.

My gratitude practice did not make me feel *happy* in the moment, but it did allow some inner relief, a sense of calm. Redirecting your thoughts during very troubling and negative experiences can keep the anxiety or depression at bay long enough for you to get through the experience and get to the other side.

This practice works in any difficult part of your life's journey: divorce, betrayal, disease diagnosis, professional or financial failure...the list goes on. And it helps exponentially if you have been developing your gratitude muscles in your everyday life. It makes it a little easier to see through the fog, to reframe the experience, and to find actual morsels of, if not positivity, ways it could be worse—and that is a welcome reprieve.

If you find yourself in the worst of moments, feeling absolutely engulfed in the pain or a sense of tragedy, just pause and look around you. Find things to be grateful for in your actual physical surroundings. This has a way of pulling you back into this moment. I can see that flower blooming in my yard, and for that, I am grateful. I am very grateful that the sun came out today after three days in a row of clouds and rain. Noticing something positive in your surroundings takes your mind away, if only for one single moment, from the all-encompassing suffocating agony of the difficult time you are in. There are times in life when getting even one single moment off the focus of the pain or of the loss, brings relief. Shifting your focus in this way gets you through THIS moment, then it's on to the next.

When gratitude is used to get through really tough times, it can act as an ointment for the raw pain at hand. It does not allow an escape hatch, unfortunately. You will still need to feel and process the painful experience. Healing takes time. Gratitude works to neutralize moments where the distress or anxiety might otherwise overwhelm you. Gratitude can act as a shock absorber when you hit those big life bumps.

As a lighter example of my personal experience with gratitude as a practice, one time on a holiday, I waited two hours for my carryout order at a restaurant. Literally! Placed my order, went to pick it up, and waited almost an hour curbside. These were the days when restaurants were adjusting to pandemic protocols. Eventually, along with other people waiting in the parking lot for their orders, many of us decided to go inside the restaurant to see what the issue was. I waited another hour in the lobby/hostess area. It was crowded, we were in uncomfortable face masks, and it was getting hot in there with all of the people. I heard voices of complaining. I heard employees scurrying around in distress, trying to determine what order went where. It was at this point that my mental and spiritual baseline of gratitude kicked in! I found myself in a situation not uncommon in life in which I could not control what was going on *around* me, but I had full control of what was going on *inside* of me.

I began thinking, *I really am grateful I do not have to work on this holiday. I have empathy for these employees busting their butts in an obviously overstretched system that isn't working. I'm grateful that however long it takes, at least I do not have to cook or clean pots and pans today! I really, really was not in the mood to cook and clean.* I was thinking how great it was that the restaurant was even open on a holiday—how convenient for us! I was thinking how I had a filling breakfast that morning, and now I just had to stand there while someone else prepared a delicious meal for me—so many others in the world, even in this country, are not so fortunate. I was thankful that I had the funds in my account to get the food. I was just standing there, unbeknownst to anyone around me, lost in my internal la la land of gratitude!

Can you see how as much as a negative thought can spiral you down and give birth to other negative thoughts: *Why is this taking so long?*

What's wrong with the management in this place? There is NO WAY it can take this long! Can't find good service anywhere anymore...blah, blah, negative blah! So too, can a grateful thought lead to awareness of another thing to be grateful for in any situation?

This practice is real. It really does work. I could've wasted two hours of my life getting my blood pressure up, fuming, contaminating the room with my negative energy and commentary, and my stomach so tied in knots that I would not even enjoy the food once I did get it. Instead, when I left, food in hand, I went home with the family and enjoyed the meal—as present and happy as could be!

As with any failure of service, this situation still needed to be dealt with. The gratitude I felt did not make me suddenly burst with glee for the wait or the inconvenience! I did, on the following day, reach out to the manager via a very calm phone call to express what I'm pretty sure was his 100th complaint about the day prior. The terrible lapse of service was satisfactorily resolved with him issuing me a gift card for a future visit. A resolution I was happy with. All was well. As you can see by this relatively benign example, a 21st century problem, a spiritual practice practiced, and *BAM,* I experienced zen. Even right there in the crowded restaurant lobby, even in my high heels!

As you are incorporating this fundamental practice of gratitude into your daily life, here are a couple of exercises you can use to bring attention to and hone your skills. First, as a beginning exercise, go to the fresh produce section of your grocery store. Stand with a good overview of all of the fruits and vegetables. We are so accustomed to rushing through the store to secure what's on our list, we take for granted what is right in front of us. Take a deep breath. Look at the miracle of all the colors and all of the textures! Wow, to think this occurs in nature! Now take time to consider the actual workers in the field who planted, tended to, and harvested all these fruits and vegetables. All day every day, working to keep conditions stable enough that the fruit and vegetables can grow. Imagine the truck drivers who pick up and haul and then deliver the fresh produce to this store. Bring to mind the produce manager and local employees who received the food, priced it, and placed it on shelves or refrigeration units for you to view!

God allowed so many processes to be in place for a tiny little seed to grow, be picked, be washed, be hauled and to be displayed right here in your own neighborhood grocery store for you to see and to choose in this moment as nourishment for your body. Bet you never felt so much gratitude for a carrot before! Have you? This is only one example. Now try it, and then as you go about your life, look for all of the other places where, if you would just stop, breathe, and be present with what IS, you will experience awe and even more reasons to be grateful!

The second exercise I suggest for increasing your gratitude practice is to write a thank you note to someone. Not a text. An actual note. Take the time to write an old-fashioned note! Think of someone to whom you are grateful—either for the role they play in your life, or for a specific act of generosity they bestowed on you. Even a local business owner: you can express your gratitude for how their company is so convenient for you and enhances your life in some way.

As you pick out the note card, or the paper and pen, you will have a lightness about you, knowing this is something special. It is meaningful to you as you think about and write about your gratitude. And as you can imagine, it is meaningful to the recipient, as it is highly doubtful that receiving a thank you note is part of their everyday experience!

When my daughter was still young, but old enough to write, I always had her write her own thank-you notes for her birthday gifts. Even if the list was a long one, I made sure she was in a state of mind to actually be feeling the gratitude she was expressing! I needed her to understand that this was not simply an etiquette task that needed to get done. This was a meaningful communication of appreciation. Not all kids, after all, receive gifts on their birthday. We talked about reasons to pause and acknowledge the generosity and acts of love she was receiving with each gift. I am hopeful she will continue this practice well into her adult life, as she has now experienced for herself how gratifying and heart-filling this easy, inexpensive gesture is!

Expressing your gratitude in a written note is good for your soul. The blessing to the recipient is icing on the cake, as you have no way of knowing how much it might touch their heart in return. Maybe they are having a bad day, or a bad week, or going through a private struggle. Your note could absolutely brighten their day and more importantly their spirit!

Being acknowledged is one of the deepest forms of human connection. God forbid something happens to the person who received your note (people do die unexpectedly every day). Imagine the peace in your heart, knowing for certain that this special person knew how much you appreciated them. A much different feeling than, *I hope she knew,* or *I wish I would've told her.*

So if we are talking about adding meaning to your life, expressing your heartfelt gratitude to another person will definitely do that. A thank you note really does *feel* good! And aren't we looking for practices in life that genuinely make us feel good? Especially a practice as easy and inexpensive as this is to implement! The late motivational author William Arthur Ward said, "Feeling gratitude and not expressing it, is like wrapping a present and not giving it."

You might be surprised in doing this exercise that you think of more than one person whom you could bless with a personal note from you. Try writing one to get the ball rolling. I bet you will feel better afterwards. A simple act you can do to contribute to your zen today.

It is important to emphasize that practicing gratitude in these ways, or in *any* way, is not merely a nice theory, but an actual tool. Gratitude raises your emotional state. Being grateful makes everyday life feel less burdensome. There are well-known scientific studies that regular thoughts of gratitude actually have the power to impact mental and physical chemistry. Gratitude has the power to improve your physiology!

As it is said, "where attention goes, energy flows." And since your mind can only think one conscious thought at a time, all the additional moments you will spend being grateful will impede on some of the negative, victimizing, *why me* mentality going on in your head. You will find you complain less! And our world could use one less complainer! Your family could use one less complainer! And your mind could use one less thing to complain about! Yes! Amen! Hallelujah!

As a hack, for perspective when you catch yourself in a moment of feeling like there is absolutely nothing to be grateful about in a terrible situation, ask yourself this question, *How could this be worse*? He lied? At least you found out about the deception before investing another ten years with this man. You find yourself fifty and single? At least you are not seventy and single. Someone died unexpectedly? At least they did not suffer—ask someone whose loved one suffered for three long years about that. It could be worse. Your house burned down? At least you are alive, and your pets are safe; it could have been worse. Be grateful for the simple fact that it could have been worse in some way, and was not. Start from there. It always works. No matter how bad it is, it could have been worse.

You will find gratitude improves most any scenario, softening the edges of the difficult moment you may be in. As you experience glimpses of gratitude in moments where it didn't exist before, it will then expand into hours of feeling more grateful than before, which expands into days, which turns into weeks, which turns into months, which turns into years. Your life will improve. And as I mentioned, *think* the grateful thought and then actually *feel* the positive emotion that the gratitude evokes.

Have you ever heard the saying, *"I am beyond grateful?"* BE BEYOND GRATEFUL! Go beyond the auto-response or the mental thought of what you are thankful for...*feel* the gratitude. Things to be grateful for are all around you, just waiting for your attention. And, as promised, like all spiritual practices, you incorporating gratitude is not dependent on anyone else! No one else around you needs to be practicing gratitude, or have any certain attitude in order for you to feel grateful in this, or *any* moment! And, like other spiritual principles, it's free!

As with meditation, there are many other books that address the positive mental, physiological and spiritual effects of a regular gratitude practice. There is not a lot more to define about gratitude here, except to state clearly that in order to be really transformative and effective, it needs to be practiced every day of your existence. Eventually it will become second nature. Your default will be to look for things to be grateful for.

You will notice as we go along our journey of discovery of essential, basic tools for zen, no one else can implement them for you. I can buy an app to help me meditate, but the app cannot meditate for me! The same is true for gratitude. I can hire a personal assistant to do a lot of things, but, no matter how much I am willing to pay the assistant, she or he cannot come up with the things my mind and my heart have to be grateful for! No one can feel gratitude *for* you, but you.

So the original theme continues: it all comes down to YOU! The reality of your personal responsibility is evident at every turn on your path to growth and transformation. Your zen, or your lack of zen, in your high heels is on YOU. Seems to suck at first, because it's natural to want someone to lean on, or conversely someone to blame, but it is, at the same time, so very empowering and freeing! It's up to YOU, and you can find your way, no matter what anyone else is doing or saying in their life! Want your life to be filled with GREAT-ness? Fill it with GREAT-ful-ness!

Meditation: check. Gratitude: check. You have laid the foundation for your spiritual journey to zen. Now we will proceed with the next spiritual practice: INTENTION.

CHAPTER 7

Intention

"When your intention is clear, so is the way."

—ALAN COHEN

*a*s promised, meditation is inseparably linked to every practice that I recommend in *Zen in High Heels*. Being in the space of silence with your Self is critical for the authenticity of how you show up and how you move forward in your life. To recap the process so far, meditation facilitated you becoming more aware of your true Self and of issues that may need addressing. Then as you incorporated gratitude, meditation allowed you to expand your gratitude into more areas of your life, and at the same time, feel it more deeply. Your gratitude practice allows you to pay more attention to the world

ZEN IN HIGH HEELS

around you in ways that contribute to you being zenful. Now you are ready for the life-changing question: *what is my intention?*

Because meditation enables connection with the true You, you will gain understanding of what your deeper self needs and longs for on her quest for expression. And, so it is also in meditation that you will be able to answer the question, *What is my intention?* This simple, honest inquiry will yield a revelation of deep truth for you about yourself. You will gain understanding. You will gain understanding regarding your actions, choices, and words from past behavior. Your actions, choices, and words for today then become more clear. You can identify your intention both in the immediate moment, and in the long term. This was, and continues to be, one of the most profound principles on my personal journey.

Intention alleviates confusion and potential anxiety over making the *right* decisions along your way. It does so by instilling new clarity. What to do or say next is not so confusing now. If certain words or actions are not in alignment with the intention you identify for yourself, you do not say the words or do the actions. It is amazing how powerful and life-changing this is. In every scenario you will be less conflicted, as the intention you have identified for yourself eliminates the guesswork.

It doesn't happen overnight, but the inner peace available to you when you move at an intentional level in your life is truly amazing! When you begin the practice of seeking and understanding your intention, you gain a steadfastness and assuredness that enable zen to reside in your mind and in your heart. It feels like a miracle! And just like other spiritual principles, NO MATTER WHAT ANYBODY ELSE DOES, the zen you feel and peace you experience from a place of intentional decision-making is yours to claim!

You can find the philosophy behind intention written about in many books that teach the path to enlightenment. In *Zen in High Heels*, I want you to understand that identifying and acknowledging and expressing within yourself and in your life, your core intention in as many situations as possible, will be an absolute game changer on your path. Clarity has never been so clear as the moment you begin operating from an intention-directed place of decision making for yourself!

What is intention? Is it like a goal? Is it interchangeable: my intention IS my goal? My goal IS my intention? *My goal is to get the promotion, my intention is to get the promotion?* Not exactly. Intention is more accurately explained as identifying what desire is *beneath* the goal. I have a goal of getting the promotion. My intention is to provide more financial stability to my family, or possibly it is to retire early to enjoy my golden years. My goal is to run a 5K. My intention behind the goal is to physically feel good and to be able to be active with my kids on family vacation. My intention is to be a healthy mom, so the 5K training goal is in alignment to facilitate that.

In one way, intention seems like a simple concept. But for the purpose of your personal and spiritual evolution, the principle and practice of intention is actually a very, very deep one.

In his book *The Seat of the Soul,* Gary Zukav declares that our, "Every action, thought, and feeling is motivated by an intention." That's quite a proclamation! *Every* action, thought, and feeling? Wow! I guess we should take a look at ours, to make sure we know what it is!

Spiritual teacher, Wayne Dyer, penned an entire book about it: *The Power of Intention*! In which he writes, *"when you activate it* (intention) *you'll begin to feel purpose in your life and you'll be guided by your infinite self."* Intention gets the heavyweight title of being an undeniable factor on our path of spiritual growth—incorporating conscious intention cannot be over-emphasized!

Let's say you want to be a medical doctor. You search your heart for your intention. Do you want to be a doctor specifically because you watched your uncle suffer and die from lung cancer? Do you feel your work as a doctor might allow you to be part of finding a more effective treatment, or even finding a cure and allow you to be a meaningful part of other's cancer journeys? Or do you have a completely different intention of wanting to be a doctor because you saw the earning potential in *Forbes* magazine?

Maybe making a lot of money does seem like the intention–but underneath wanting to earn a high income might be an intention of escaping from the roots of poverty you grew up with. Wanting a six or seven figure salary might be feeding your desire for respect, for power, or your desire to feel safe, a safety that you believe financial stability will give you. Intention is what you believe you will experience in your life as a result of achieving your goal. In this example, it is safety and security that you are seeking.

Maybe you've never thought about it. Do think about it. Get intentional about your life! Sometimes identifying the underlying motivation or desire of the heart will awaken you to move in a different, better-suited direction for your soul. Moving in a direction more in alignment with your soul will *feel* better. You may realize you were a passenger on the train of society or on the train of your parents' desires. In this case, you may have unknowingly been acting on an intention of not wanting to disappoint your family. Being a passenger on the train someone else is driving will never ultimately lead to your potential or your zen. Operating from an intention of fear—*I don't want to let them down*—is not the place you want to be. Look to discover, *What am I seeking from this experience?*

The spiritual part of intention versus a goal is that a goal is to do "X." At the end, you know whether or not you did "X." "X" is measurable. Intention, although it directs behavior, action and words, is additionally a *QUALITY*. Identifying your intention brings the energy of the true You to the equation. Acting with intention brings a consciousness in your words and deeds. Unlike a goal, the outcome of intention driven behavior may not always be outwardly quantifiable. You may or may not achieve the goal, but you will know if you acted with intention, and towards your intention, and *that* ends up making all the difference in your experience.

Without consciously identifying your intention, you can reach a goal and still feel completely unfulfilled and empty. But incorporate intention in the process of seeking your goal and you will feel satisfaction. You can feel the growth forward, even if you do not achieve the desired outcome yet.

Additionally, working spiritually from a place of intention allows you to be present along the way as you work to reach the goal. You can close your eyes at night with satisfaction and even peace knowing that no matter how much closer you got or did not get toward the intended goal, because you have identified your intention and acted accordingly, your words and actions line up with and support your true, deepest desires. You are laying the groundwork for success, spiritually speaking. Like your gratitude practice, incorporating intention FEELS good. That internal feeling contributes to your zen each day you live in accordance with your intention. It makes your day feel meaningful in a deep and pure way. Unlike anything you can get externally.

Intention acts as a binding agent between thought, word, and action. Clear intention lays the path to value driven decisions. Thus intention solidifies integrity in you. Life feels good in the space of personal integrity. This creates its own reward system for you internally. So it doesn't always matter the actual outcome of the external circumstance; you will know who you are and why you are doing what you are doing. There is an undeniable sense of assuredness within your Self when you incorporate intention into your life. All is well.

As you begin to practice, even if your newer intention-guided choices do not seem to make sense on the outside, you will still feel a sense of positivity. As I mentioned, without intention, you may do the action, and reach the goal, but feel perpetually unsatisfied or empty. Intention allows you to realize that you will be good because you know you are on the right track, no matter the outcome. Intention works like gratitude, in that as you progress in your practice, it becomes second nature to ask yourself in everyday situations: *What is my intention here?*

Bring actions, words, and choices in line with your intention and feel an authenticity in the way you move through your days and weeks. Intention is a principle that can be used for the big and for the small things. In a big thing like motherhood. Determine your intention for your role as a mother. Then, act accordingly at every crossroad. Your intention will then dictate your choices based on your values. Actions based on your intention become not merely a nice idea, if circumstances make it convenient, but rather, your resolve. You may have to say no to some opportunities; you may have to sacrifice at times. But these choices will not feel tumultuous. When you are clear on your intention, it drives you toward the greater good. You can surrender to that and feel a beautiful, well-earned sense of satisfaction and inner peace.

While it's true that intention does contribute to your peace *in spite of* the outcome. The caveat is that, especially in regard to relationships, intention does not necessarily mean things will turn out the way you desire. Intention brought to difficult relationships or interactions with another alleviates the need to anticipate other people's words, actions, or reactions. It takes the things you cannot control out of the equation; at least in terms of wasting your mental space, time and energy, because you are now clear about your own thoughts, feelings and behavior.

Intention creates clarity within your Self. There is way, way, way less ruminating and replaying conversations or interactions that do not go as expected. Were you clear with your intention? Did you speak and respond based on that? Good. (Or if not, make note and do better next time.) You cannot control how someone else speaks or responds. Intention helps navigate what are ordinarily complex interactions with other people in difficult interpersonal relationships and gives you a sense of peace knowing that you acted clearly with your intention in mind.

I cannot tell you what your intentions should be. Nor can anybody else. This is for you to seek and discover within your Self. Seek and listen to what the underlying true desire is for you in life or even in the next conversation you are getting ready to have.

With that said, your intention never involves another's behavior. *My intention is to get him to stop drinking.* No. Your intention might be to not enable or to not be a contributor or supporter of the denial going on around that person and alcohol. That would be a healthy intention.

My intention is to beat Bob in the race. No. Your intention is to leave no stone unturned in your training, diet, and schedule so you perform the absolute best possible for you that day. And, as a bonus, you will probably beat Bob.

And I can tell you that pure, soul-origin intention is never negative. *My intention is to destroy that company or that person.* No. This would be a desire of an egoistic mind. Not an intention of the soul. I can also tell you that you have limited power to intend for an entity like the business you work for, or for the evolution of a relationship. Your true intention is not to keep the company from going bankrupt or avoid divorce at all cost. Your intention in both scenarios is to show up to the best of your ability, in your truest state of wholeness, to make the bankruptcy or the divorce less likely, or at least not a result of your neglect or sabotage.

You can only be the best you, and trust the Universe will protect or dissolve the business or the union—whichever is in your best spiritual interest in the long run. The Universe supports your evolution in this lifetime. How many times did we think the job or the person was what we needed, only to discover months or years later that the undesired outcome of a breakup served our growth? Even during trying times such as these (pending bankruptcy or divorce), we can continue to seek our intention, and count our blessings along the way.

When you know you have spoken and acted in accordance with your intention, even if others do not respond as you desire or are not in cooperation, you will find, if you are patient and determined enough, that if you combine intention with continued practice and growth using other spiritual concepts, eventually your life looks like, feels like, and reflects your truth. YOU can show up! YOU can shine! Intention is especially powerful in illuminating your path to zen in situations where you find yourself feeling conflicted. Like ROCK-PA-PER-SCISSORS, intention trumps desire or goal, which are oftentimes ego-oriented. Intention becomes what you put your attention on when things feel rocky or uncertain, helping you feel more stable and secure. Intention can be a beacon of light when your path feels dark or unclear.

When you are able to identify the big picture or the end goal, you are not so easily distracted or discouraged by every bump along the way. How much more secure and calm would your life feel if you were operating this way? Clear intention gives you inner fortitude and strength to say NO to things that you really want or need to say NO to.

Let's look at an example of how this can work in a scenario that illustrates what might ordinarily cause inner conflict and stress and may even cause you to deny your intention in order to not look like a bad person. Let's say you have decided it is in your best, highest interest to keep your Sunday evenings free. You've decided not to go anywhere or do anything social with the intention of showing up to work on Monday more fresh and productive than you have been. You have an intention of being the best, most productive employee you can be to your company and/or your team. And now, one of your good friends, or a family member asks you to commit to their recurring charity volunteer position on Sunday evenings.

Here is a situation where you can practice incorporating your new understanding of intention. You want to honor what you feel is a clear intention: staying home on Sunday evenings. But in the same breath, you can see that your friend or relative needs you. After all, you think, *What kind of schmuck would say no to feeding the hungry children (or whatever the worthy cause)?* Decisions such as this do not require you to disregard your intention. Depending on the specifics of all variables, you may decline. Or, you can decide it is not abandoning your intention by offering your time this next Sunday since she is in a bind. But after that, you let her know that you will not be able to help, but you will absolutely reach out to help her find someone else who can help on future Sundays. You are only slightly modifying your intention about Sundays (offering one Sunday), AND at the same time, you are not leaving your loved one high and dry at a time of need.

Another option, especially in regard to charity invitations, is if it does not work for you to go, you can politely decline, but let them know that you will make a donation to the event or cause. Sometimes this is what the asker is looking for: reaching out to people in their circle to make a difference for the charity. If you are unable to donate your Sundays, let your friend know you are going to donate some money or food/clothing items (or whatever the need is) on her behalf.

Someone who is not consciously engaged on her spiritual growth path, who is not practicing intention-based decisions, would very easily get derailed by the request of the friend, despite just three days ago telling herself she would not book her Sunday evenings anymore. And, because she is not intentionally using intention, she will feel she has no choice (because she does not want to disappoint her friend, and because she wants to not be a schmuck in the eyes of anyone who would find out she declined to help a charity), the power is not hers—or so she thinks!

When you are operating without clear intention in any situation, your choices and behaviors are open to moment-by-moment interpretations of what to do next. This allows the weaker, ego-driven decisions a chance to play out—leaving you to question later, *Why did I do that?* It is difficult, if not impossible, to live in higher consciousness without clear intention.

When you are living with intention, you can derive inner satisfaction in situations that previously gave you extreme anxiety or mental turmoil. I know this for sure from personal experience. It takes a level of patience and a level of maturity to let this principle and the rewards of it lock in for you, but once it does, you will have an unshakable understanding of who you are, where you are, and of what you need to be doing precisely at any moment. Operating your life with intention alleviates guesswork and anxiety.

Once you get clear, and set your intention for a specific circumstance in your life, you must then begin to pause. You must be willing to look truthfully and be honest with yourself. Take space to notice when decisions you make, actions you take, or words you speak are not in alignment with said intention. This is an example of identifying the gaps we spoke of earlier. Find the gaps and then work to bridge them. Narrowing those gaps creates growth you can see, and you can feel. This is the deep and personal work of the principle of intention.

Integrity is one of the things you will discover in the process of navigating your life with intention. When your heart, mind, and soul are in unison, your words and actions are no longer dictated by what others bring to the table, but rather they become in alignment with your truest Self. You begin to say what you mean to say, and do what you say you will do. This is the place from which you begin living with more inner peace.

Being intentional enables integrity. The integrity that comes with intention brings the zen. Zen shows up for you. Your mind and your heart and your life are in harmony. Most likely not 100%, but it leads the way as you continue to learn, to grow, and to evolve. You cannot be acting based on the deep integrity of who you are, of what your intentions are, and feel confused, anxious, and stressed. You cannot. Confusion, anxiety, stress, or any negative emotional state does not reside in integrity and intention. This is not perhaps your initial definition of integrity—of, say, being a "good person." Integrity in the spiritual, human potential realm is *integration*. The integration of intention, action, and word. When you learn the truth of who you are, your words, actions, and decisions are in alignment with that, THEN you are living in integrity. Even in undesirable circumstances, when you act in alignment with your true Self, inner peace abides. Get intentional about your intentions, and you will find each day begins to be filled with satisfaction and an excitement in anticipation of what tomorrow might hold.

You will come to see the integration of WHO you are with the decisions you make, and with the words you speak. The integrity of your actions create a well-tilled, well-fertilized soil for your life. From a place of integrity, you are no longer blocking the sun, but open to receive it, and the most beautiful, bountiful harvest of the spirit you can imagine will bloom. Integrity: authentic expression in words and actions is what creates an internal peace and confidence, upping your zen factor exponentially!

Let's look at another common scenario that may have been causing ongoing distress for you and how you can apply intention to it. How do you use intention for attending a family gathering in which you have a history of problems or drama with a particular family member or two? Decide in advance, with assistance from your meditation time, your intention for this event. *It is my intention to show up to spend time with, and in support of my aging parent. It is in line with my intention to be polite but not engage past politeness with the troublesome family member(s). I will conduct myself in a way I see as proper. I will conduct myself in a kind, calm manner, which is a true representation of who I am. I have taken the time beforehand to acknowledge for myself that through politeness, I am not plugging myself into any drama, nor am I conceding to the other person's previous or anticipated bad behavior. No matter what anyone else chooses to say or do, I am clear as to why I am there. I will fulfill my honorable obligation to my parent, and equally importantly, to my Self.*

Can you see how my heart and mind can actually be calm on the day of the event? Negative emotions subside because I have created true meaning around my reason for attending the family gathering. The anxious, restless thoughts around anything I cannot control have subsided. I know who I am, and I know why I am there. THIS IS THE POWER OF INTENTION.

Now, to continue with this example, as we know, we cannot control any "others." If I show up, and am confronted or egged on in an aggressive way, I can choose to leave. Not because of a threat I feel from them, but because my intention was to show up to support my parent and to be polite. I've done both of those things. I choose to leave now, not because they have run me off; I leave because I choose to remain in the realm of my intention by doing so. Engaging in a cycle of argument would only pull me out of my intention for this event, which was to be calm, kind and supportive.

Or, in this example, if my truest intention does not allow me to attend the family event, I must honestly and openly communicate my intention of seeing/honoring my aging parent on another day. And then I must follow through with that intention and promise to my parent. If this is the case, you will be able to decline the event, not to "teach them a lesson," but rather because you have learned yours. You know what is healthy for you to accept, and you set boundaries accordingly. The cool thing is that boundaries set in line with intention then free your mind. If you do not go, you will not be thinking about it all day. You will not waste time wondering who is talking about you, or what they are saying. It doesn't matter.

I hope you can see, from this very practical example, a shift occurred. I did not leave the function because of them, nor did I necessarily

ZEN IN HIGH HEELS

decline to go because of them. I actually gave the power of choice back to myself. I chose to act in accordance with my established intention. There is a calm resolve within me. It is different than in the past. I am different. Zen can find me now. Zen did not stand a chance of finding me the way I was operating before, from a place of constant REaction of others' words and behaviors. I was operating from the unconscious pattern established long ago, not from a conscious, intentional place of present Me, who has identified her own true intentions much of the time.

If something specific regarding the gathering is brought to your attention, you deal with that then. Otherwise, what is happening there is none of your concern. Excuse your ears. If someone reaches out and tries to pull you into any drama, you may reply, "If Y would like to have a conversation with me, I am open to that, but I am not interested in gossip or third-person commentary on what transpired."

I can already hear some of you thinking, *Well you obviously do not know **my** family* or *This would never work in my situation*. OK. If you want to argue for why you cannot respond in an evolved way, you win. Every time you argue for your limitations, in any scenario, you will be awarded that victory. These principles, or any other principles, will not be able to override a closed mind. You may not yet know anything other than being triggered and reacting to what others bring to the table. It might feel impossible to imagine another way. But I promise, there is. What happens when we continue to do things the same way, but expect or hope for a different outcome? Oh yeah, insanity! It drives us crazy! Clearly not literally, but also clearly, your path to zen will be limited if you allow others—*any* others—to be a block in your road.

Please don't say, *But I feel guilty.* There cannot be guilt. You may very well desire a relationship with everyone involved. But your intention only allows you to invest in reciprocal, healthy, emotionally nourishing relationships. This means the ones that do not meet that criteria must take a back burner for now as you are seeking to make your own life better. We only have a certain amount of emotional energy in a day, so you must not dilute yours by focusing on the people who do not have your best interest in mind.

Others can only impede your progress when you are a willing participant. As Eleanor Roosevelt so famously said, "No one can make you feel bad without your permission." Perfectly said Mrs. Roosevelt, thank you! And as enlightenment teacher Ram Dass is quoted, "You think you're enlightened? Go visit your family." Ha!

If you believe intention-driven words and actions will not work in a long-standing family or even work situation, continue to practice your spiritual principles in other areas. As you continue to evolve and get stronger in other areas of your life, eventually you will be better and stronger at implementing your intention in difficult situations. You will have skills and a better understanding of what words of truth you need to express in order to change your part of the dynamic of the troubled relationship.

The only thing you have control over is you being true to YOU. Because I know I cannot control anyone else's behavior, and because my intention does not involve anyone else's behavior, I am now free. I am completely free from arguing with, trying to reason with, or gossiping about how any other person or people act or speak.

If you have a history of constant bickering with that "difficult" family member, coworker, or person, just stop it. Choose to stop it. Think of it as raising your outlet. What I mean by that, is you can be clear within yourself at what level you choose to engage. If they usually plug into you with their words and inevitably try to evoke guilt or drama for you, just move your outlet higher. Really, if they plug into the outlet that normally sparks your head spinning and your mouth defending, but this time the outlet short circuits because there is no power there—because you made a conscious decision to raise to a higher outlet and not engage in the same way—things will change.

Your energy and focus are freed from previous patterns of toxicity. You may not be as close to the person in question as you once were, or think you should be, but your life will eventually become more open to the other relationships around you which are available to support you. And like I mentioned before, you being different allows the possibility now for the relationship to change. Keep your heart open, as it is possible that ultimately, your relationship with the difficult person will get better. When they don't have access to your power source anymore, they may be able to evolve to a more productive way of interacting with you. Just don't engage at the same level. Starting today. Don't even announce your decision, just be different.

What an important, pivotal piece of advice! This alone can alleviate a significant amount of drama or suffering for so many of us. Choosing to move your outlet to a higher space will minimize frustration for you in reoccurring difficult interactions with another person. It is what it is, and they are who they are. You do what you can do, you change what you can change. The theme of self-understanding and self-adjusting continues! You get to play the lead role in your life now!

I do understand, and I am definitely guilty in my past of caring too much. I understand the longing for a healthy, loving relationship with all of your family members and people you engage with—feeling it should just be natural to love and support each other, to GET ALONG! I spent many years trying too hard and wanting things to be right. When they weren't, it really, really bothered me. I took the disappointments to heart, which left me wallowing in pain and confusion or jumping through hoops and doing metaphorical backflips in an attempt to make things better. Realizing only now, as I have evolved through the spiritual principles, that when I pour my energy into my side of the equation whether things work out or not, I have peace.

There was a burden of carrying more than my share of the load—no matter how great or loving I believed my motivation for doing so was. I can move more freely and in more productive ways now. I choose to only carry my part, which is really all I could do all along. But now I am living in alignment with that reality. I am living in the reality of what actually IS—not me trying to make things what I would wish for them to be! Other principles that we have yet to cover aided me in my evolution in this regard. But INTENTION is where healing and inner harmony begin. There is no longer angst and strife in my mind! All is well.

If you are open to imagining the possibility of a different reality, starting with YOU, there is hope for change. Sometimes you will find that instead of trying to tolerate the person, or trying to pull off something that goes against your every fiber by faking it, as you act with pure intention, you may very well set the stage or space for true and honest communication to occur. AND FROM THIS PLACE, perhaps genuine healing and restoration with the other person(s) will occur. At least now there is potential for a different and better outcome. If you do not react, or if you react differently, it changes the equation. Act in integrity with intention, and see how much better you feel. See how much more energy you have for the things and the people who offer support and nourishment to you.

Practice this concept, seek your intention, and find the power in letting it guide you. This allows your life to be different and more zenful. No matter how long it takes, if you are different, your relationships will eventually be different too. In time and with effort, you can apply this principle in any complicated relationship scenario.

The principle of intention is applicable at work, with the neighbor, the social acquaintance, and yes, even with your mother-in-law! Is your mother-in-law really an OK person, just not to you? Decide you want to attend and be polite for the sake of your children having a grandmother, or for your husband to not feel the stress every single time you have a family function with his side. Put any mental grievances or your mental scorecard aside, and act according to your intention. Watch your life get better. Enjoy the blossoming fruits of this spiritual practice as you see the ease and benefit in the lives of your husband and children also.

Pay attention. Observe how interactions with others unfold. Begin to notice where maybe your actions or your words aren't in direct alignment with your intention. It's tricky. Some things are very obvious. And some things are not unless you look for them. You could say well, *this was my intention*, but *he did this*, or *she said that* to me to provoke me and make me respond this other way. No. You act from your intention always. Strive for that anyway.

The more and more you act and speak from your true intention, the more the outside world presents to you what is in alignment with you and when it does not, you will be able to care less and detach from the expectations you once held. Not care less, as in you do not care anymore about the person, rather, you put less care and concern into their actions and words. You keep the love in your heart for them, because love does not dissipate, but you love them from afar if that is what needs to happen to keep your own peace and your own integrity.

Fortunately, there is more to come regarding this not uncommon experience of complicated relationships. We will delve even deeper into what seem like difficult relationships and how to maneuver our way through them to find our own growth. But this truth will not change: do what action allows you to act in line with your intention and the pitfalls and the drama will be minimized!

Deepak Chopra teaches that most of the conflict—maybe even ALL of the conflict—we experience with others stems from a place of not understanding or appreciating the fact that the other person is just acting out of their current level of consciousness. Understanding this, accepting that the other person is acting out of their level of consciousness does not make their behavior any less annoying or even acceptable. What it does do, is give you a new level of compassion, so you are more easily able to let some of their words or behavior roll off your back. Let grace fill the space and see how this changes the dynamic of the relationship.

This is not to say a toxic, rude, and disrespectful person gets a pass. No. This is just to say, or to bring to your attention, the fact that oftentimes a "difficult" family member or work associate actually is not truly toxic. They are probably just unconscious and trapped in their way of being, which has nothing to do with you. Perhaps he or she is just not capable of facilitating the kind of relationship that WE would like or they are not filling a role, or a need that WE think they should. What if you can look at your mother-in-law, or any other person you want to remain in a relationship with, but you experience as difficult, with a filter of LOVE? Imagine a bright filter around them (like people use on Instagram), softening the image of the difficult person that your heart sees. God loves them as is; maybe you can love them too.

Perspective allows for presence. And maybe, just maybe, a change in perspective can allow for tolerance? But in the case of true toxicity or disrespect, you choose not to engage, or you reach out with the idea of family therapy or the idea of changing departments if this is at work. You must begin with presenting your side of the equation differently, but ultimately if it comes down to making a choice—acting in accordance with who you are, or acting against your truth in order to sustain the relationship—YOU MUST CHOOSE YOU. Each scenario will be different, but I have confidence if you are putting the other tools to use, you will find your way.

This principle of intention in action may sound simple or even obvious to you. I am certain, especially in the beginning of your evolution, this practice of identifying and operating with intention will not be an easy one. This is where the waters of spiritual growth appear murky and can feel almost like quicksand. As the deeper part of you is seeking to make itself known, perhaps for the first time, it can feel extremely uncomfortable to both you, and to the people you interact with the most in your life. As you realize ways you were not speaking or acting that would actually facilitate realizing your intentions, the new road will feel bumpy.

Depending on where you start, and how far off you've been living from your truth, it is a process that will take time. Many components may need to fall into place, and there will probably be several lessons for you to learn along the way to realizing your deepest, truest intentions. Take this tip: as you notice times that your words or actions are not in alignment with your core intention, you will usually find that FEAR is the motivation behind the misalignment.

Not speaking or acting with direct expression of your intention in hopes *they* will like you. Or in hopes they won't really see you, and therefore, they cannot really judge you. Or in hopes that you will not have to claim responsibility for your life. A weaker version of you can cower to the outside pressures and influences and, ultimately, the FEAR of any repercussion of you actually being YOU.

It is because, in the beginning, lining up your words and actions with your intention may not feel safe, that seeking and trusting and acting on intention is such a feat of bravery. You will find some relationships implode, some explode, some slowly dissolve, and some relationships will just need to be different. It is OK. If this happens, it is just your life lining up. You are cutting the tethers to the old, less truthful, and less peaceful You. You will have more room to attract healthier relationships and heal and strengthen the ones that do continue.

Brené Brown, vulnerability teacher, uses this concept as a definition of courage. "Courage is showing up 100% even when you know you cannot control the outcome." Be courageous, show up authentically, knowing you have no control over the other person or the eventual outcome. Be courageous even if it means you will disturb the previous status quo. Do not give up. Stay with the process. Keep being intentional and showing up. It does work, it does get easier, it is not for sissies, or everyone would be operating this way! You can do this. Integrate as many of the other spiritual practices as you can, and be

patient and kind with yourself and with anyone involved as you practice aligning with your intention.

If you are not experiencing zen, you must embrace change. Changes
that occur as a direct response to you being truthful and intentional
always make way for your path to zen. The yellow brick road to zen
is paved with your honesty and your integrity.

Intentions run broad, and, at the same time, can be very specific:
you can identify your intention for your new year's resolution, for an
activity you are involved in this weekend, or even for a conversation
you plan to have today. This is true for your job, how you handle
your neighbor, and even how you manage your schedule. Evolving
intentions affect who and what you say yes to. Intention is the core
starting point for improving your life—relationships and otherwise.
Every area of your life has an identifiable intention underneath if you
look for it. Know that intentions are not carved in stone; your intention will probably evolve and refine as you go. Always be willing to
revisit and question your intention for yourself. Since intentions are
formed from your current level of consciousness, as you grow along
your way, we anticipate your intentions will be evolving and expanding with you.

As I mentioned, I do not have specific advice for you on what the next
right thing is for you to do in any scenario, but intention will help
your decision-making process, because it narrows the options to
only the one or ones that are going to get you closer to your desired
intention. If you are honest in seeking your intention, you will know

which next decision is in your highest interest. This is how clarity shows up for you! The correct choice or action for you is now clear, or certainly more clear than when you operated without conscious intention. In being able to identify which choice(s) are not in line with your intention and eliminating those as options, you embody less fear or confusion. When you use intention as the filter for decisions, you will not choose the absolute wrong way street—metaphorically speaking. You will not veer too far off your path because undesired results of that will steer you back and have you checking in with your intention for clarity.

If you have your intention set, but you do not have clarity about the next step to take, my advice is to look at any actions you are taking today or in the near future and eliminate anything that is keeping you farther from the intention you desire. If you don't know clearly which way to go, become proactive in ways that are clear for you *not* to go. Choosing not to engage in sabotaging or distracting actions, relationships, projects, even conversations is sometimes equally as important and powerful toward your growth!

Intention is very, very deep. Identifying your truest intention requires you to search and to be very honest with yourself. If there are times when it seems you have conflicting intentions, *I want this, but I also want to stay in the relationship,* then you have not gone deep enough.

More surface-level desires might disguise themselves as your intention for a while. These are parts of the ego consciousness intending to keep you on a "safe" path. Intention is the FORCE behind the goal or the desire. It comes from deep within and is centered around your core values. At your source, intention never conflicts. At the level of the mind, or level of the physical, it may look conflicting, or yield what you thought was an undesired result, but with time, you will see the purpose for which things played out the way they played out. From this place of decision-making, your life, as mine did, will undoubtedly change for the better.

It is all good. No need to worry about getting this step 100% accurate. Start small; start with something that makes sense to you. Just be conscious, start with an intention for TODAY and see how this change in awareness gives meaning to your daily decisions, your daily conversations, the daily things you give your time and attention to.

By the way, intention does not replace goals. I continue to have goals. Challenging yourself and striving toward goals is important and adds to your vitality! Intention actually helps with goals, because one of the naturally occurring by-products of acting with intention is discipline. You become more precise with where you put your energy when you understand your intention. Discipline becomes a necessary component to aid you on your journey. It becomes clear what to say YES to and what to say NO to. There is no negative connotation in regard to discipline now. People often ask, "How do you remain so disciplined?" Operate in intention and see for yourself!

Just keep all of your spiritual work as your foundation so as you journey through your accomplishments and your goals, you bring with you your TRUTH and your integrity and a more enlightened version of yourself to the victory! Then you are much better equipped to be present and enjoy the accomplishments! When you embody integrity, the achievement of any goal is magnified.

You making an effort toward living with intention sparks hope and joy in your soul. As your soul now plays a role and is no longer being neglected for what it can contribute to your life experience, you will become grounded in a way that others cannot disturb or steal from you. Again, piling on the probability of zen for you!

CHAPTER 8

Words You Speak

"Let your words elevate your life to the heights of greatness."

—BUDDHA

The next principle to support your effort towards zen is to be VIRTUOUS WITH YOUR WORDS. Not far behind the power of thought, is the power of word. "Words spoken set your life in motion," is the first declaration to an extraordinary life in Michael V Ivanov's book, *The Mount of Olives*. Words we speak originate as thoughts, so it is an indication, if our words are causing trouble for us, that we need to look closer at our thoughts. Noting yet again that meditation, taking time to connect with our thoughts, also plays a supporting role here in this principle of accepting and utilizing the power of the words we speak.

As one of the *Four Agreements*, Don Miguel Ruiz states this concept as: "Be Impeccable with your word." "The word," Ruiz declares, "is not just a sound or a written symbol. The word is a force." And quoting psychologist and empowerment teacher Jordan Peterson, "You have no idea what will happen to you if you tell the truth. If you're looking for an adventure, tell the truth."

Sounds obvious. Sounds simple. Just don't be a liar and you will be fine. But wait—back it up! What about the little white lies? And, is there a difference between an outright lie, and withholding speaking your truth? As you go throughout your day, you will be shocked by what this concept reveals to you. And how often we fall short!

Do you mean what you say? *I'm starving!* Are you, in fact, going to starve? When you are stuck in traffic: *I'm dying here!* Are you actually going to die? In an argument, *You ALWAYS*. Do they *always? You NEVER*. Really, is this true? *Never, ever?*

You may take this in gist and say, "Well, you know what I mean." Maybe I do sometimes, but maybe I don't sometimes. Maybe the person listening does or maybe he or she does not. Maybe your subconscious mind does not either. And your powerful, in-charge-of-default-mode subconscious is listening to every single word you say! You reinforce your reality with the words you speak. *I'm never on time*. Is this the reality you want to reinforce? Pay attention.

It is really good practice to start noticing within your own mind if your words match what you mean. You may be quite surprised. *I'll call you;*

we'll do lunch! Is this true? Do you know that you will not call and that you have no desire to ever go to lunch with this person? Then don't say it! These half-truths or complete non-truths add up. They chip away at your integrity. Both with the person whom you spoke the untruth to, and, equally as important, with your Self.

Being impeccable with your word cleans up your lane and keeps it clean. Your lane being the part of the relationship or conversation that you have control over: your words. As mentioned, integrity is one of the things you will discover in the process of navigating your life with intention. Words should be a verbal expression of your intention; allowing for you to have that integration of thought, WORDS and actions. Being impeccable with the words you speak contributes to your integrity and unclutters the path for moving forward.

Being truthful with your words builds an internal trust with your Self. This reliability creates personal confidence. You can be more confident because you have nothing to hide. When you operate from this place of honesty and authenticity, it frees you up for things like vulnerability. Meaningful conversations and feelings of connection require honesty and vulnerability. More of this way of communicating = more zen and more connection for you. One of the very beginning points we made about engaging on your spiritual journey, was the desire for each of us to show up for our lives. We want to fully show up for our lives and for the people in them. There is no better way to achieve presence and availability with others than to operate from a place of honesty and communicate that with your words!

When your words do not line up with what you really think or believe, you create a gap. Zen cannot be found in the gap. This is another one of the gaps we spoke about earlier when we were initially trying to understand what we were doing to cause the absence of peace and zen in our lives. And, if there is a gap between what we really believe and what we speak, as expected, we get to claim responsibility for it. We created it. No one else is doing our speaking for us. Bridge the gap. Speak words of truth. You reinforce your reality with the words you speak. You will find attention to the words you speak has probably been underutilized on your path to living your best life.

We get more specific about the Law of Attraction later, but on a quick note, if the Universe is listening and responding to the things we think and say, is it any wonder why certain particular drama seems to follow us? Do we take every opportunity to re-tell the story of our woes? It's like feeding the weeds and then wondering why the weeds won't go away! How much longer does talking about being the victim keep you in victim mode? Do you continue to talk about how wrong the other person was? How wrong the circumstances were? How can you possibly move forward when you keep reminding yourself and anyone who will listen how wronged you were? You are probably correct; it was not a good situation, it may not have been fair, and they did do you wrong. But if you desire to move forward now, you must start putting your thoughts and your words toward the future, toward what it is you want to build for yourself. If you need help to do this, get it, but do not be the barrier for yourself to grow forward by continuing to be careless with how you speak, and what you speak about. Your next adventure is waiting for you.

We know how powerful words are just from our own experience. Someone, some adult when we were a child, some teacher in school, some relative, an ex-love carelessly directed unkind, not necessarily true, words at us that stuck. We've all experienced being on the receiving end of negative words spoken to us before we knew any better than to accept them as valid and accurate. Recklessly spoken words do have the power to affect our emotions, our confidence, and even, ultimately, our beliefs about what is true.

Just as the wrong word spoken by the wrong person at the wrong moment can have a profound and lasting effect, so, too, can the right word spoken by the right person at the right moment have a profound and lasting effect. The teacher, the coach, or parent who said just the right words of encouragement to empower us on our path when we needed it most can have a huge impact on our ability to see ourselves as worthy of achieving success.

Take a moment to realize as the speaker, you, too, have that kind of effect on others with the words that you say. Since you've read the principle of gratitude, I know you are now practicing it, which has led you to use your words to complain less often. Now you can add to that by looking for opportunities to use your words to encourage and edify others in your life—even strangers who cross your path! Can you offer a compliment? Can you seek out those doing a good job and tell them so? Words can be very powerful. Let's give our words the attention and respect they deserve, and use them to make a positive difference for ourselves and others. When we are speaking words of integrity and positivity, we create an environment where zen thrives!

Do not make the mistake of underestimating this critical principle of paying attention to your words in your ability to have healthy relationships. We all know you cannot un-say something mean or hurtful that may have been uttered in a disagreement. THOSE WORDS DO NOT MAGICALLY DISSOLVE when you calm down. I learned somewhere that it takes seven good, kind, or positive phrases to undo or lessen the severity of one harsh, critical, or hurtful phrase!

Think before you speak. Take a breath, take space if you are seeing red. How many relationships are damaged or ruined by unintentional words, by exaggerated half-truths spoken in anger or offense? How many texts do you wish you could un-send? This is such a perfect scenario if you struggle with it—to realize something deeper may be triggered to cause such un-lovingness from you, who, at your core, is absolute love. Search for the reasons within yourself. No one can cause you to blow up. Really, there is always a choice. If you feel otherwise, seek professional therapy or anger management classes. Get to the root of your inability to express yourself and speak phrases of truth versus using your words as weapons. Be impeccable with your word. This will change your life.

Additionally, in terms of the power of our words affecting other people, we must refrain from gossip. Keep yourself out of other people's business. There is no pure intention in gossip. Even if we are certain we know something is true, we do not know all the elements involved. We are not walking in anyone else's shoes. Your words about someone else's situation to a third party only add fuel to the burning, negative, out-of-control flames engulfing them at this time.

As the Bible says in Proverbs 26:20: "Where no wood is, there the fire goeth out: so where there is no tale-bearer, the strife ceaseth." Most of us have been on the receiving side of gossip where someone was speaking about or judging our private business. It evokes pain and frustration, because they really have no idea what you're going through.

Do not succumb to the enticing temptation of gossip. Gossiping only serves as a distraction and a hindrance to your own spiritual path. Stay busy minding your own business, tending to the work you are doing, not letting the path of another distract you. Do not use your precious gift of speech on a damaging, low-vibration activity like gossip. Gossip does not contribute to your more peaceful heart. Get involved in a messy situation of another, and now your name and your energy are attached to it. As Pastor and author TD Jakes says, "People who live on purpose don't have time to meddle in other people's business." Be someone who lives on purpose, with no time to meddle in other people's business!

Another example of how our words have power is evident even in how we speak to ourselves in times of illness. There is an amplitude of science and research on this topic that our words can affect healing or lack of healing. If you paint yourself a victim with no control over your own health, your body cells, your brain and your nervous system tend to believe you. This is not a book on physical recovery from symptoms or disease. But please, if you are suffering or struggling in this regard, do research on the miraculous mind/body connection in regard to healing. Neuroscientist Lisa Feldman

Barrett has scientific research to support the power of words on the human body, proving that words can actually affect heart rate, hormones, immunity, and more! You re-enforce your reality with the words you speak.

Scientist Masaru Emoto has a very well-known lab experiment with water where, in summary, they took microscopic photographs of water drops (specifically the crystalline structure of the water drops) and then exposed the drops to control groups who either directed positive or negative words and thoughts toward the water. When they re-photographed the water, if it had been exposed to praise and positive thoughts and words, it was brilliantly full, bright, and perfectly symmetrical snowflake looking. Contrarily, if it was spoken to negatively with words of hate, it looked shriveled, unsym-metrical, dark, and overall unhealthy. Stunning! Real and scientific. Please, please do not disregard your words as a significant contrib-utor on your journey of self-actualization, expansion, and health! Be kind to yourself and others with the words you think and the words you speak!

Many times, this principle of being virtuous with your words will have you speaking less! You will find unnecessary words and unnecessary half-truths become: unnecessary. You might even realize them as an interference to your growth. You will become aware of when refrain-ing from saying something is the appropriate way to go. Instead of speaking an untruth, or speaking words of truth that will have a repercussion that does not align with your intention, you can choose when to be silent. Yet another place where the ball is in your court.

You get to choose, and you hold the power in this regard: over your tongue!

As you continue to grow on your spiritual path, you will find that the words you speak tend to have more meaning. The things that you say become more meaningful because they are a truer representation of who you are and of who you want to be. It is a naturally occurring positive repercussion of your work. When you speak in truth, your truth, and with regard for your intention, your soul rewards you with an increased sense of peace. More peace equals more Zen! Speak truth. Speak love and light into those you encounter: claim zen! You won't be perfect, but I hope you will WATCH YOUR MOUTH! I know that I am watching mine!

PART III

Navigating the Bumpy Road of Relationships

CHAPTER 9

Personal Responsibility

"It's not you, it's me."

—GEORGE COSTANZA

Unless you have moved to a mountain alone, or joined a monastery, just sitting with your meditative, grateful, intention driven, truth-speaking self, is not realistic. Much of our life is spent moving about in the world and interacting with other people. Our relationships with others constitute a huge part of our life and our growth. Being able to navigate relationships is intrinsically woven into our path to enlightenment. Relationships with others allow us to fully express our souls. Our relationships give meaning to our lives and serve always as a reflective barometer to help us learn what we need to learn along our way.

As you incorporate meditation and the three tools from section two: gratitude, intention, and honesty in your speech, your relationship with yourself will undoubtedly change for the better. How these changes affect our relationships with others is where so many of us get stuck. We realize we are not able to move freely or peacefully within the proximity of certain people in our lives. This is usually where we experience the biggest divide between who we aspire to be and the reality that actually plays out.

An understanding of how spiritual principles apply to the relationships in your life will serve to disrupt unhealthy patterns that have been prohibiting you from actualizing your zen and will increase your ability to better connect with others.

Before we proceed, understand that the principles we will discuss in the next few chapters are intended for you as an adult to help guide you to make your relationships, and subsequently, your life better. Understanding and practicing these principles will move you out of emotional suffering, turmoil, and continual drama with others. The caveat to each concept is that if you have had any kind of inappropriate, immoral or illegal behavior or abuse forced on you by another person, know that I am in no way suggesting the responsibility of that or attraction of that to you is something you deserved or that you could have avoided. In such cases of abuse, please take these principles as tools to help you move forward from any wounding that was instilled in you by the trauma. Getting yourself help now and doing the work to heal are what become your responsibility. You can break any unhealthy relationship patterns that may be occurring as a result of underlying pain these experiences no doubt caused you.

Ready? Let's get started. We begin by exploring the principle of personal responsibility in relationships. Personal responsibility is the understanding that at the core of any relationship, or any relationship issue, is the full acceptance of the part you played (either consciously or unconsciously) as a contributor to the dynamic of the relationship. Even though by definition, to be in a relationship there is another person involved, we need to seek understanding and change from the vantage point that we can ultimately understand and change: our own. To be enlightened, to know zen, the blame game stops here.

In seeking to better understand the relationships and relationship problems we find ourselves in, we have to be willing to look at our part of the equation. We need personal accountability, because as soon as we put 100% blame on another person, we essentially turn over all of our power to them. In order to create something different, a different dynamic within our relationships, or different kinds of relationships altogether, we must get to the place where we are willing to ask, *What is my part?* No matter what your relationships have looked like up to this point, one thing is clear: YOU have been the common denominator in all of them!

Ask yourself and genuinely seek to answer these questions: *What part did I play in the relationship problem? What behavior did I allow that has now contributed to this relationship problem? How could I have better communicated, or listened, or not reacted, or trusted my intuition that this was not the right friend or partner for me all along?* And ask yourself, *What is the lesson in this for me? Why has this person or this experience in context with this person or people caused me such angst?* If you're having a problem that just won't go away, you have to figure out how you've been feeding it.

All of the aforementioned questions and resulting insights are driven by YOU. The other person is merely a variable in the equation. The truth is that the solutions you seek are not dependent on the other person(s) in any way. You get to take back your power! I realize this is not as simplistic as it sounds, so we will continue to cover in detail how to apply personal responsibility and how to navigate our way as we piece it together with our understanding of the other relationship principles.

Personal responsibility as a relationship principle is not a new concept. Deepak Chopra and many other spiritual teachers expound that relationship dilemmas are never really about the other person with whom you are having the dilemma. Deepak actually cites ALL relationships are simply a mirror, reflecting something back for ourselves to see. Ouch Deepak! *ALL* relationships? Even the negative, closed-minded, pompous neighbor who I cannot get along with?

I have not yet evolved to understand this concept all of the time in my own journey. So for now, I give it the 80/20 rule. 20% is or can be about the actions or words of another. Maybe they are being difficult or maybe their behavior was morally wrong, their words DID hurt my feelings. But then comes the part that, especially in the beginning of your journey to consciousness, is more difficult to accept: that 80% of this problem I am experiencing is on me. *If another person says or does something that is absolutely wrong, how on earth could it be any kind of reflection of ME? I am not the one who did anything wrong!* Stay with me on this.

We put the words and actions of others toward us through an internal filter, where we attach particular meaning to it and then decide how to respond. This is so often the point where walls of defense come up: we are justified in our reaction, no need to dig deeper. Our ego has made it clear: *they* were obviously wrong!

What they said or did may have indeed hurt you. To grow spiritually and emotionally, you have to be willing to look closer. Ask yourself WHY? Why do you feel hurt? Search for the why, and then for God's sake, DO NOT argue with it, deny it, or dismiss it when it starts to reveal itself to you! Be willing to look at the truth, at your truth. Sometimes if you are willing to look deeper, the answer is not what you might have been expecting. The other person made an off-handed comment, but when it went into your internal filter, the comment reminded you of the bully in third grade or the time when you failed at something and felt publicly humiliated. The current-day comment was benign, but not to you! Your ears and your heart heard and felt the words differently!

Any unconscious barriers that have kept you from taking personal responsibility in your relationships, the ones that justify you staying in blame or victim mode, are not going down easily! It is at these critical junctures when you are yearning to understand or change something in which you have not previously taken the time or awareness to step back and evaluate, that the subconscious tactics to keep you from growth flare into full force!

Your subconscious, ego defenses will give you a million-plus-one reasons to: (A) not deal with it now! You are too busy, it is too stressful; it is not that important to understand; just dust it under the rug like you usually do! Or (B) remind you how bad or wrong the other person is. Clearly you are not the one at fault here! Or (C) instill fear in you that you might not be capable or worthy of clarity and the responsibility of setting boundaries that clarity would require, or the growth that will happen when you do!

However, because you are now seeking zen in high heels, you are not giving in to these types of previous unconscious excuses! You are now choosing bravery and growth moving forward in your life. So let's get back to our question: WHY? *What is my part* in a seemingly negative or uncomfortable situation with another? Beyond the obvious answer that they acted as a jerk, if you want to break relationship patterns for yourself and find your way back to zen, you must look further. Did you get hurt because:

- you overinvested in the relationship with a built-in expectation that the other person would be willing to or able to reciprocate, often overlooking "red flags" to the contrary along the way? Is this revealing a recurring pattern that you have an unhealthy tendency to not look at what IS, but rather what you hope it will be?
- the infliction reminded you of how you felt as a child or in a previous relationship that caused you pain and triggered that unhealed wound to surface?
- their words or behavior represent something you would NEVER, EVER say or do, or be, thus revealing to you a part of you that has been hidden, or denied, or shamed, known as your shadow side. If you can stuff or suppress this in yourself, why can't they? Absolutely unacceptable! Your ego mind says.
- the Universe is giving you an opportunity to practice what you have been learning on your spiritual growth path. Here is a seemingly difficult but all too familiar situation, pattern, or person: what are you going to do (or say) this time? This could be your chance to see it differently. Did this person CAUSE your insecurity? Or did he or she REVEAL your insecurity? Instead of being the victim of it, become a beneficiary of it. So much power in this concept.

Law of Attraction supports this premise that we, ourselves, are responsible for everything in our lives, including our relationships. The Law of Attraction teaches that relationships and interactions with others occur not randomly, but instead, as a reflection of our thoughts and beliefs, which attracted these people or circumstances to us.

The Law of Attraction is the Universal law that like attracts like. Teaching that everything is energy and that the power of our thoughts, along with the energy and emotion attached to those thoughts, creates a vibration. This vibration is what draws circumstances and experiences to us, like a magnet. Somehow, for some reason, we have attracted this messy or undesirable relationship or situation for ourselves. Again, reinforcing that although there is another party involved, we can claim personal responsibility for the origin of the relationships and relationship problems we experience. "You're the magnet, the other person is the mirror." Nicholas Ashbough, YouTube Lightworker.

Basically, the Law of Attraction teaches that we create an energetic vibration with the cycle of thought-emotion-thought-emotion and then that becomes the reality we experience. I have this thought that brings up an emotion that re-affirms the thought that solidifies the emotion, and on and on and on. The Universe responds and gives us evidence of what we have consciously or unconsciously decided we can expect.

Let's say we have a belief: men are not faithful. According to the Law of Attraction, we will then attract men who will confirm and verify that belief. Without consciously realizing it or not, this very powerful Universal law is giving us exactly what we are believing exists:

unfaithful men. And, should an actual faithful man get in our way, we will just self-sabotage so that he goes away, and we can get back to finding what we set out to find: an unfaithful man.

The unfaithful man brings us proof, *I knew men could not be trusted*! This allows the thought, emotion, and observation cycle to become even more deeply embedded and invade our belief system. If our life or part of our life is moving in a direction that is working against our zen, the Law of Attraction can be like a vicious cycle of observing and reacting, which re-affirms the negative thing, causing repeated negative consequences. That is until we bring awareness to it. Until we ask ourselves, *Where did this thought originate?* And until we challenge it: *Is this actually true, are there no faithful men in the world?* And then we learn to replace the thought, (if we so choose) and reprogram our mind, which will certainly change the vibration we put out into the world. Turns out, finding a faithful man was an inside job. We used faithful as an example, but it could be violent, angry, insensitive, emotionally unavailable—any undesired attribute.

There is a school of thought that if we experience an emotionally painful event—say unfaithfulness—but do not healthily or adequately deal with the pain it caused, it remains unhealed in us. Our subconscious then continues to look for a similar experience to replay in hopes of a different outcome. If we are experiencing something or someone negative, we can assume personal responsibility for our part by looking closer, by digging deeper to understand our contribution to creating this scenario. We can reflect on what it is IN

US that attracts, or is attracted to these men (or people, it does not have to be in a romantic context).

Sometimes it is hard for me to wrap my head around this concept regarding a particularly difficult person or painful situation, and how I "attracted" that to me. But when I remain open to the possibility that I could, indeed, create a new set of circumstances by setting my thoughts and attention in the direction of my desire to attract something different, I feel empowered. When I am open to the possibility that I drew a seemingly negative experience or person to me because I am now ready to observe it from a spiritual perspective and learn the lesson, it becomes less burdensome: *Why me? Not THIS again*, but instead more inquisitive, *What is this here to teach me? What truth does this reveal about me?*

Remember it is HERE, in the willingness to be open and in the space of awareness around an issue and your relationship to it, that growth may occur. *This* is principle number one: Personal Responsibility. Be willing to take ownership of the quality of relationships you have and watch as you grow out of the ones that do not suit the newer, truer version of you.

Utilizing the Law of Attraction for the purpose of growth is NOT just switching out a negative thought for a positive thought—the power of positive thinking philosophy. The mind is incredibly powerful; being positive and thinking positive thoughts is very important to your vitality. No argument here. But what I'm expressing through the Law of Attraction and personal responsibility, is that you think positive, you dig for what you believe and why you have that belief, and then you do the work to heal any underlying issue or wound. You challenge a negative emotion or experience, not deny its existence. This is the part of the process that requires bravery. "A spiritual warrior must have the courage to face and accept the death of their beliefs." Gary Van Warmerdam, creator of PathwayToHappiness.com.

Deep-rooted issues that are behind our beliefs, issues such as fear, abandonment, and unworthiness, do not go away because you choose to ignore them and "think positive." Each infraction you have experienced, past or current, that you think you are pushing away by denying it or not thinking about it, is still in you, fueling negative beliefs about yourself, or about others. You may think you are ignoring past experiences that breached your trust or caused you pain and confusion, but in actuality, they lay idle in your subconscious, waiting for a chance to make themselves known, usually manifesting in very unhealthy, sabotaging ways to get our attention. Deep-rooted unresolved pain or trauma like to make themselves known, especially in our relationships.

It's no one's place to tell you what these micro or macro traumas are. It's up to you to search your heart and mind for times, big or small, when you were wounded or neglected intentionally or unintentionally. It is important to be really honest with yourself when identifying these things that need your attention. Do not judge or justify occurrences because your logical mind thinks they may be too small or insignificant. *I know _____ happened to me, but it only happened once.* Or *It could have been worse—other girls experienced and survived much worse.* Or perhaps if a parent left or betrayed you in some way, do not say, *At least they did not physically abuse me—only verbally.* Or *at least I had one very good parent or other relative who stepped in.* Yes, it is an excellent practice in gratitude that things were not worse. But the fact still remains that at some point in time, on some level, you felt traumatized. This or these experiences must be acknowledged for all the feelings and fears and subsequent survival techniques they instilled in you and in your subconscious moving forward since then. It is up to you to look for ways this undealt with pain might be manifesting in your life today. Only you can dig up the feelings and seek this understanding about your Self.

Some of these issues may reveal themselves in meditation; some come up just by observing patterns in your life. Any undesired, especially re-occurring undesired circumstance or emotion, is evidence that something else is trying to get your attention. You must be willing to search. See it, feel the feelings hidden there, process it, and let it go. Doing the work of understanding where this re-occurring issue is coming from is so valuable. If you can identify the origin of it—like a shadow on the wall that looks like a monster—you can realize it's causing unmerited fear or fueling behaviors in you to avoid it. When you realize it is indeed just a shadow, you can handle it when it shows up. Acknowledging the thing you are afraid of or avoiding means you do not have to react the same way now. You have identified it which lessens its capacity to negatively affect you and your life.

You begin to heal the lingering effects of trauma by acknowledging it. Acknowledge that it did happen. Acknowledge the truth of how it made you feel. Acknowledge the ways that the unresolved painful event of the past is affecting you still today. Do you constantly feel a need to protect yourself? Do you overcompensate in some other unhealthy way? While healing trauma, get angry if you need to, grieve if you need to. Feel the feelings, cry the tears, acknowledge the pain or the disappointment the breach of trust caused your heart. This is part of your emotional history. The fabric of your emotional self may be unraveling, or bound too tightly because of it. Look at all circumstances and parties involved from your now older, wiser perspective. Release it by accepting the strength it gave you. Set an intention of moving forward with a new sense of freedom, as you are now working toward setting free the part of you that has been held captive.

While it is true that the acknowledgment and the processing of the pain does not erase it from having happened to you, or erase it from your private history, it does release its power. The power the trauma had over you by forcing you to hold on to that secret, by instilling fear, confusion, or unworthiness in you that does not belong to you. Acknowledging the pain in this way can be a starting point from which things can change. Unacknowledged pain can feel like quicksand from which you are using all of your energy just to avoid going under in any given moment.

All of us have issues to resolve, it's just part of the human experience. Some issues are obvious and traumatic, some very much not so obvious. Usually people in our lives will trigger us, continue to wound us, or enable us to stay disabled in our pain until we break free and get healthy. It's important to understand that undealt with negative emotions are always limiting to our growth and often eventually turn out to be destructive to our relationships or our lives.

Attempting to get to the bottom of relationship problems with the lens of personal responsibility (perhaps for the first time, ever) is another one of the points along the way of growth where you may benefit from a good therapist, or energy worker to help you unpack and process any new realizations and unhealed emotional wounds that surface. If you haven't sought out support yet, now is the time to consider it. There are many therapies and modalities available to assist you in the process of releasing past hurts or traumas. Do some research, connect with a therapist, or find a professional organization that specializes in supporting people who survive your particular trauma. Do whatever you can do to support yourself, because you are worth it.

Recurring negative, drama-filled relationships are a sure sign for you that there is deep, personal work to be done. Work that really does have nothing to do with the person or people with whom you've been engaging in such an unhealthy way. Please hear this! It does not matter how pure your intentions are, or how bad and awful the other person's behavior is, a cycle of bad relationships is a reflection of issues for You to resolve.

Unexplored patterns remain just that...PATTERNS. Something that repeats itself. The relationship, the person, the circumstance will not change itself. Or, like the earlier example, you dump one cheater, only to go find yourself another cheater. That is until you do the work. Until you learn, and change, and move yourself forward! Reclaim your power in the situation! Move forward in the direction of a different, better future.

You may wonder, *Why would I want to relive or face old pain?* It sounds so unpleasant, even excruciating! The answer is because in doing so, in doing the deep work of your life, on the other side is not only the healing of those past wounds, but is also where you will find FREEDOM for today. You will find personal emotional FREEDOM. Personal emotional freedom allows you to draw to you healthy, reciprocative relationships. You will be able to experience FREEDOM today from ongoing cycles of drama. FREEDOM for your future! Freedom to bring a healthy, available, authentic version of you to relationships. Being vulnerable will feel like something you are willing to risk. You will feel safe! Something valuable is waiting for you on the other side of the pain.

Let's say for the purpose of demonstrating this point that somehow you were previously hit by a gunshot and the bullet lodged itself in your midsection somewhere. At the time the incident occurred, for whatever reason, you did not have access to a hospital. The bullet remained, but your open wound from it eventually healed up, so you could not see the scab or the bullet, and you went about your life.

The prevailing issue now is that you have had to adapt to what it means to have a bullet in your mid body. People who meet you cannot see the bullet, or the wound. But you've accommodated the bullet, it is now part of you. Your digestion is disrupted—but you've grown accustomed to this. You have sharp back pain if you twist a certain way, but you are used to that too, so you just try not to twist in such a way that you can feel it. Even certain waistlines on clothes aggravate the entry point of the bullet.

Now you can certainly go about your life in this manner, with these limitations. Most people around you won't know any different. Or at some point, you can opt to temporarily reopen the wound to remove this painful reminder of the day you were shot. Now, however, it is a more mature You choosing to deal with the bullet once and for all. Now, you can get professional help with the matter. Yes, for a time you will need to take it easy. You will be perhaps in more pain as the bullet and possible scar tissue are removed. No doubt the day of removal and the days that follow, you will experience more pain than the years, months, or weeks leading up to the extraction. In time though, everything heals up. Your digestion improves, you are free to twist and bend whatever way you want—but now pain-free! Even the waistline on clothes becomes a non-issue, giving you unlimited choices on what used to be limited.

It is an important part of the journey of living to your potential, to remove the metaphorical bullet, but it is a *choice*. You may certainly choose to convince yourself that the bullet is just fine lodged there for this long. After all, living with limitations has become your norm. You have become comfortable with the limitations from the original wounding. You are just fine.

Consider any bullets you have endured. Consider the traumatic wounding left inside of you because of them. Meditate on the issues that you may have been suppressing. In the privacy of your mind, in your own time, eventually you will probably come to realize that it is time to go deep and remove the bullets. It is time now to heal and to regain freedom from whatever ways the presence of a bullet or bullets have been limiting you and inhibiting your growth!

This removal of what was blocking you opens the door for the possibility that all the qualities you long for will now be available. And, you will finally be able to sustain them like never before. Zen in high heels will be yours! This work, this spiritual surgery of sorts, is part of your journey to zen. There is no emotional scarring so big or so deep that it is unable to be healed. Issues such as yours have been healed in others. The good news is that you will be so much stronger both because of the bullet, and because of your willingness and bravery to remove it.

Buddhists refer to this process of looking deeper into your pain to heal what is there as digesting and assimilating the original and subsequent wounding. In emotional digestion, you take what you need (what nutrients the experience has to offer you) to learn and to grow and thrive, and you can then eliminate the rest of it. What was once a recurring theme is no longer an issue for you. You got what you needed from it and you are one step closer to enlightenment.

The revelations you receive about yourself when you choose to be aware and more conscious will evoke a newfound understanding of what is in you that needs healing. If you can observe yourself: your thoughts, your words, and your actions in relation to others, you will begin the process of understanding your role and your responsibility in those relationships. If this awareness allows you to create enough space to react better and differently even some of the time, with some of the people, you will become empowered! When you start the process of realizing your own power, there will be no turning back to the way things used to be!

Part of personal responsibility means controlling what you have control over. In addition to what you say to others, another thing you can claim responsibility for in relationships is how much you listen. Listening is a massively underutilized tool in relationships. No one can listen for you. You get to decide each day, in each conversation, how much you are willing to listen. This decision will change the way you show up for others.

This seemingly simple skill of listening will facilitate more under-standing on your part of others with whom you are in relationship with. And I think we can all agree that being understood and seek-ing understanding of others is certainly a positive aspiration for improved relationships. People will reveal their truth. Be willing to hear it. Truth about a person is revealed in what they say and in what they do not say. In spiritual growth, we're always looking for truth. Be willing to acknowledge what that is. No matter how you want to rationalize or make excuses, TRUTH IS TRUTH. As you begin to pay attention and to listen, you may discover things that could save you some heartache down the line.

In some instances, actually listening with the intention of hearing, nets a positive result. When you allow someone to be 100% who they are, and you are coming from your place of being who you are, one of the absolute most beautiful of human experiences occurs. You are able to meet in a sacred space of deep intimacy. It's the connection our souls aspire to, especially with those we love, but is often so rare to experience. When you do your inner work, you find that you position yourself in such a way that you are in alignment for this true intimacy to occur more frequently and you will be surprised that it can happen at the most random times, even with the most random people. When you show up authentically, you create an environment for others to do so also. Listen; allow space for others to open up. See how this improves your relationships. Talk less; listen more. If only we had a Fitbit for our daily word limit!

Being willing to look at yourself and accept personal responsibility for the ways you attract and contribute to the dynamic of the relationships you are in, gives you insight that can change your life. You will gain insight as to how and when you have been giving up your power to others. THIS will make zen available to you. Every day. Even on difficult days. Even in the 21st century world of stress. Zen in high heels is found, as you become aware, as you practice and as you build on each spiritual and relationship principle for yourself.

Let's move on to the next healthy relationship principle, the principle of Non-attachment.

CHAPTER 10

Non-Attachment

"It is not the outer circumstances that entangle us. It is the inner clinging that entangles us."

—LAMA SURYA DAS

The Number One agreement for spiritual peace (from Don Miguel Ruiz's *Four Agreements*) is to not take things other people say or do personally. Teaching that we cannot attach our mood, or our worth, or surrender our peace, to someone else's behavior toward or observation of us. Ruiz's first agreement supports our relationship principle number two: non-attachment. Let's explore how this plays out not only with our romantic partner, but in all relationships.

You may have heard the sentiment: *your opinion of me is none of my business.* This is a big one. Someone else's perception of or action towards us feels personal, but it is not. We cannot attach significant meaning to words directed at us by another who attempts to steal our inner peace. I love that part in the movie, *You've Got Mail*, when Tom Hanks' character puts Meg Ryan's family-owned neighborhood bookstore out of business with his large corporate bookstore, and he tells her, "It's business, it's not personal." To which she responds, "It's personal TO ME." Damn, I feel you Meg! I hear the spiritual teachers say that it is NOT personal, but sometimes the words or actions of another DEFINITELY feel personal TO ME!!

In addition to not holding on to and not giving any real meaning to another person's opinion of you, or words toward you, non-attachment means you detach yourself from the expectation of a particular outcome that is beyond your control. Attachment to specific outcomes creates the majority of relationship discord and is the origin of most relationship drama. Attachment plays out as blaming, manipulation and dependency on another to be what we believe they need to be, say, or do. Attachment sucks the joy out of us.

It is not literally being attached to another, as in commitment or marriage. We are speaking of the attachment in any moment within the relationship to a specific outcome, spoken or unspoken, which you have decided needs to be in place or occur in order for you to be happy. This is another way that we relinquish our power to another person. Attachment makes it easy to step out of your intentions and your values and allow someone else to determine in this moment how you feel: good or bad. Almost by default, attachment is anxiety-provoking—as you are waiting for another's actions, words, or mood to dictate your next action, words or mood. Because you have no power in this scenario, anxiety is born.

An unhealthy pattern of attachment might look something like this: I respond to what you do, without consciousness on my part. You do A, I attack. You do B, I bolt. You do C, I use that as an excuse for destructive behavior—I drink or eat too much in response. If you are not happy, then I feel like I cannot be happy. I do not claim responsibility for my response. It is predicated on what you say or what you do. *If you would not have done that, I would not have had to do this. It's your fault. You caused this mess.* If this sounds familiar, you might consider doing some research on codependency. There is no zen, I am certain if you are part of a relationship like this.

Your happiness cannot depend on what somebody else does or does not do. Non-attachment releases us from the imprisonment of expectation of another. When we are attached to the behavior of another for our sense of peace, we remain shackled. Attachment creates a mental and emotional grip inside of us in regard to what another person is doing or might do. In attachment, you may fear another person's freedom to choose for themselves, so you work hard consciously and unconsciously to manipulate the way things go.

In a state of healthy non-attachment, I accept full responsibility for my current level of happiness or unhappiness. Non-attachment creates a freedom for you as you watch things unfold and resolve without getting tangled up in the elements you cannot control. You have faith. All is well. Will non-attachment make an unhealthy codependent relationship suddenly healthy? No. You two can get therapy and work on new ways of communicating and interacting, and it might get healthy. But chances are, when the magnetic force that brought you together in the unhealthy way dissipates, so might the relationship.

In the relationship arena, as with any arena of life, you must get honest about your core values, and just like we discussed before, identify your intention and speak and act based on that. This puts you in alignment with the non-attachment principle. You get to claim the part of any relationship you can control: how you show up. You always acting in alignment with your truth illuminates your side of the equation, thus allowing the potential, the possibility for the best and most loving outcome. Beyond that, you have no control. Zero. Ever. This frees your mind. This frees You.

It can be a real challenge to claim this higher perspective of non-attachment and not taking things personally, especially when the words or actions of another are actually aimed directly at you! We can take a moment to acknowledge that the negative actions of another toward us FEEL personal, but then remind ourselves that ultimately, it is not. EVER. Others are behaving out of their level of perception, and if it is negative or hurtful, it is coming from their own limits and sense of lack. They are speaking from their lens-colored glasses, which are whatever color their experiences have painted for them, which may be far from rose-colored!

Now how you choose to react to the perceived offense is indeed personal to You. This is tricky, this is something we may practice and be able to do on some levels, let's say professional, but there seems to always be someone in our lives with whom we react. We lose our sense of who we know ourselves to be, and we react, react, react! They get under our skin in that oh-so-annoying way and we get fixated on why they are WRONG, WRONG, WRONG! Especially in juxtaposition with us!

This is often the moment we like to pick up the phone and call our girlfriend or sister to divulge this latest exchange we had with the annoying and obviously wrong person. Our automatic response is to find someone we can state our case to. We regurgitate the story, tainted along the way with our personal interpretation of how terrible, wrong, rude, insensitive, and did I mention WRONG the other person is!

Let's look at the underlying intention of such a conversation. What is it you hope to achieve by picking up the phone? One thing we're probably looking for is validation. "Don't you see, and agree how wrong *they* are?"

So now what? Your ego is reinforced in its stance of right-ness. You are right—they are wrong. Tell five people. Let everyone know. Each affirming ear acts as a "hit." A hit like smokers get from a cigarette puff. A hit for your pride. A hit, really, for your victimhood. Hmmm. Is that what you are seeking? And, dare someone stick up for the other party in your story! Now you will veer off on a tangent trail of defending yourself. Lots of busyness and justification for the mind. Just how it likes it! These interactions keep your mind and life in the familiar level of chaos and stress you're used to.

There is NO spiritual growth in this very common way of responding to what you have experienced as a negative interaction with someone. Growth has a chance to come if you don't pick up the phone. If you allow yourself to sit with it. And again, inquire. What emotions were evoked? Just this small change of choice, not calling someone to vent your case, can create a shift. Make a decision to bypass your initial reaction and cue into your deeper response. Notice your urge to defend or justify, and instead, be willing to seek answers. What is at the root of your reaction? Here, again, is a real-life, practical example of a way you can create change toward your zen. These subtle adjustments of taming your reactionary mind can be very profound on a soul level.

Negativity loves to slide into your awareness and the ego will justify why it is there. Now that you see it though, you can morph those thoughts into something more productive. If you are thinking, *That guy is a jerk, and what he did is wrong.* How are you supposed to turn that around and not be provoked into a reaction? What if he really is a jerk and what he did really is wrong? Let's practice morphing this example into something that serves you better.

Start with *That guy is a jerk and what he did is wrong.* OK, let's assume that is true. AND, what else? He is a jerk, and I'm really glad I see that now, and I don't have to waste any more time in that situation. Or if it is someone you cannot avoid, you can at least change the role you play with that person. Because as they say, you teach people how to treat you by what you tolerate.

Or in this example of the guy being a jerk, if it made you really, intensely reactionary (let's say angry), think back to when you felt that way before. Who in your life treated you like that before? This may be an indicator that even though the person did something obviously wrong, it brought up in you emotions from your past, making their behavior *feel* very personal, but actually indicating you still have some unresolved things to look at that have nothing to do with the words or actions of the person you are currently in conflict with. They were just generous enough to be a jerk so your subconscious could make known an issue it is ready for you to resolve and let go of.

Look for your point of power in any relationship issue. Where is your point of choice in the scenario? By power, I mean the power you have to change your perception, your role, and your beliefs about the situation. Your power of choice is to choose what way you would like to continue or not continue with this person. How does the saying go, *It takes two to tango?* They cannot tango with you if you leave the dance floor.

Usually when I encounter a negative or rude person, I immediately think of how grateful I am that my mind is not so dark and cluttered that I feel the need to act that way too! For I know what is coming out of them is only what is inside of them. From the abundance of the heart the mouth speaks. Hurt people hurt people. A circumstance did not cause that person to spew angry words or actions, the anger was already inside, bursting for an outlet.

This understanding on my part creates space, which enables me to diffuse any reactive anger or frustration within myself as a response toward the other person. I feel space between my Self and those rude, negative words or actions. I can see pretty much immediately that it was not truly about me at all. And as a bonus of my spiritual perspective, I have empathy for them. I say a silent prayer that they will find the healing and the love they are desperately in need of. I see them as wounded and thirsty for peace, not someone who I need to defend myself against or verbally attack in return. *Give them a taste of their own medicine?* Nope, not me. I am certain that their own mind is tormenting them with many doses each day of negative, defensive, angry, impatient poison, which they in turn easily spew onto others. The justification of their ego mind for their right to be angry or hurtful keeps them trapped in their own internal prison of pain. I am, I remain, unattached to needing them to do anything different in order for me to be OK.

Before my growth toward consciousness, I would have replayed such an incident in my mind and carried it with me all throughout the day. I probably would have called someone, *You won't believe what some guy or gal just said to me.* But now, I step back, see it for what it is and say a prayer or blessing for them as I continue on with my day. It is beautiful. Zen sticks around for me, despite this encounter! This is non-attachment in action.

It's incredible, the jerks who cross our path by chance or ones we are deeply involved with, hand the ball to us with their words and actions, and then we get to respond. How we let it affect us, that choice is always ours. *BUT*, we proclaim, *he did this or she said that.* When you are reactionary, you are not standing in a place of your own power. It's like the words or actions of another uncork you, and power just drains out. *He can't get away with that!* Pause and re-direct the attention back to something you have control over: your Self. What are You doing? What are You saying? What are You allowing? If the answer is nothing, then great, go on about your day!

If this example of rude or negative behavior toward you is not coming from just some random stranger, but rather someone you are in a relationship with, ask yourself: *Is this an isolated incident or ongoing? Were there signs I missed that this person did not have my best interest in mind?* And, although they are saying it harshly, *is there any truth behind the words for me to explore? Am I having a strong reaction because of something I experienced in my past?*

Take inventory to receive the message, or to experience it for what it might be—nothing to do with you. Now you can have a conversation to get to the root and possibly heal this relationship, or you can re-examine your role with this person, which may call for you to minimize or even eliminate future interaction. You have several paths to choose which will allow you to not find yourself on the receiving end of their reckless outbursts. You won't put your trust in someone who you now know is not worthy of that trust. Or you will reposition yourself in relation to them so as not to be in their line of careless negative words or behavior! Whichever route you choose, don't minimize this point: YOU get to choose. Practice personal responsibility, practice non-attachment. Every single day the Universe will give you opportunities to utilize these important skills!

I do not want to be misunderstood, non-attachment is not asking us to ignore or excuse troublesome or hurtful behavior of someone with whom we are in a relationship with. Just put on your happy crown and be happy when your partner is disrespectful in any way? No. But being responsible for your own emotions, and not being attached to someone else's emotions allows for a healthy space between you and the other person. From this healthy space, you have a healthy perspective. You are more easily able to see the reality of the dynamic you have with the person. How many times have you been able to see an unhealthy dynamic between your friend and her boyfriend, only to have her be in complete denial? She is too attached.

When you are not unhealthily attached, you are able to have the conversations that need to be had, and you are able to proceed forward with the decisions that need to be made to honor your path. Healthy boundaries are a by-product of healthy non-attachment.

You be the best version of you each step along your way, and things, people, and circumstances will fall in place, fall in line, or fall away. You give no regard as the process unfolds. *This* is the spirit of non-attachment. You control what you can control. You. You being right with You. Non-attachment is an essential component of a healthy relationship. Non-attachment validates your faith in the Universe.

Non-attachment validates your faith in universal order. You are in alignment with the divine. You do not get anymore peaceful and zenful than that!

CHAPTER 11

Relationships as Teachers

"Every person we attract into our lives is there to move us to the next phase of our personal evolution."

—DEBBIE FORD

This ushers us perfectly into the primary, overarching relationship principle, which we have already been alluding to, which is to see **Relationships as teachers**. If you are not familiar with this principle, understanding relationships as the brilliant teachers they are will be a game changer. Relationships as teachers for our growth, especially difficult or what we perceive as negative relationships, is a mind-blowing concept!

We think, *If only he or she would do or stop doing something, we wouldn't be having this problem!* Seems pretty clear and simple. But for some reason, the other person does not or will not change, and now you seek answers. Your mind gets busy: *How can I get them to change? Or how can I get them to see my point of view?* Understanding relationships as teachers helps you turn the focus back on You. The lens you use to view difficult relationship issues becomes reflective. Being willing to step back and look at what the Universe might be asking you to see, allows you to gain the understanding and clarity you need. If the relationship distress itself does not subside, you will be able to feel less distress about it. This will give you the inner peace you seek.

In the context of relationships as teachers, could the earlier example of the jerk who hurt your feelings, have been a case of SHEEP in WOLF'S clothing? We are familiar with the phrase wolf in sheep's clothing, someone appearing good or quite harmless, but in reality being a big, bad, ill-intended, destructive wolf underneath the facade. But sometimes—many times—what we initially perceived as negative or terrible, that "enemy," spiritually speaking, when you delve below, could be exactly what you need. We might even realize it as a blessing. As big and bad as we judged this "wolf" to be, taking a second look allows us to see him or her actually as a harmless sheep, ushering in a valuable message to us.

Darren Weissman, author of *The Power of Infinite Love & Gratitude*, refers to the dichotomy of circumstances showing up in our life appearing first as negative, but ultimately being the exact right thing we need as "a gift in strange wrapping paper." As spiritual students, we come to know difficult or triggering people who are in our lives or who cross our path, as supporting players for our call to growth, embracing the principle: relationships as teachers.

In her book *Sacred Contracts*, Carolyn Myss talks in depth about this concept of people and circumstances being teachers in our lives. Myss theorizes that on some level, all of the players in our life, especially the significant ones, are working FOR us. We've basically hired them, in a spiritual sense, to teach us, to help us evolve. Imagine our soul posts a help wanted sign—HELP WANTED: personal growth department! A person or people then apply for the position to bring our attention to, and possibly resolve, what needs resolving within us. As her book title implies, when we enter into a relationship contract, consciously or unconsciously, if the experiences and emotions it gives us contribute to our evolution, it is indeed: SACRED.

A conversation I had with a client about the harsh treatment and words of her sister illustrates this perfectly. "If it came from ANYBODY else, she exclaimed, I could ignore it, but it is MY SISTER!" Exactly! If books could have sound effects, you would hear the dinging of a winning bell here! Ding, Ding, Ding!!! Your sister had to say the words or do the behavior; otherwise, it would not have gotten your full attention! The Universe now has your attention! The Universe could not use your co-worker or your neighbor. It HAD to be your sister.

Can you grasp this concept of how the ones closest to us, or who we feel may have hurt us the most, are actually acting as perfect teachers? If we seek and allow the lesson, if we delve deeper into the equation, we will learn, and more importantly, we will grow. Thank you, Sister; I will navigate my way spiritually through this. I will be open to see what it is I was not seeing before, and either we will be better for it, or I will be better for it!

Can you see how seemingly negative, zen-sucking experiences or people are not necessarily a difficult and annoying unmovable block or unsolvable problem but rather a unique piece of your soul's puzzle for you to solve? A puzzle, even a somewhat exciting adventure of discovery where I trust truth and zen lie waiting for me on the other end. It's like the children's game Chutes and Ladders, where you land on and climb the ladder to move exponentially farther on your path to victory than any roll of the dice would ever facilitate! These principles, when applied, act as a ladder, helping you grow, moving you forward on your path in ways you can't imagine. There is a challenge for you or a gift for you to uncover in *any* relationship that you are in.

Relationships as teachers is an all-encompassing principle. Teachers can appear in any relationship we are part of: deep and long-standing, or casual and fleeting. After all, every relationship I am in has the common denominator of ME. From this place of understanding, I can acknowledge and honor ALL the people and experiences of my life. Each one has brought me to this place on my life path.

Just thinking about this concept makes me smile! If we remain open to the possibility that there is a REASON this seemingly difficult person is in our life or that a person said or did something that triggered a response of pain or a negative emotion is fascinating. Considering that the Universe is conspiring for my growth, which, if I am willing to acknowledge and address the issues it brings to my attention, will ultimately lead to my freedom–emotional freedom from this issue or this recurring feeling of pain and frustration will result in peace! More peace! And zen! My zen! An entire new realm of possibility is now there: like a mystery to solve, you are one step closer to discovering that personal buried treasure of zen.

Citing Deepak Chopra again, he teaches that, "Growth is ALWAYS in the direction of greater love and happiness." I'll take that. Bring on the experiences, let me learn, let me grow, move me forward in the direction of greater love and happiness! Accepting a negative situation with a new perspective that allows me to claim some of the responsibility (Personal Responsibility principle) is actually liberating. I'm not bound helpless at the mercy of someone else's behavior (Non-attachment principle). Can I remain attached only to my own intention, remain zenful, and, if necessary, be proactive with a future conversation, versus being reactive in this moment? Can I use this person, or exchange as a catalyst to dig deeper to see what is trying to be revealed to me? (Relationships as teachers principle) Indeed evolving to this place of understanding and practice is a breakthrough milestone on any path of personal growth!

Don't get me wrong—people disappoint me. It sucks. It stings. It's not like someone behaves shitty to me, and I think, *YAY!* No. But the sting, the sucky-ness of it, doesn't last as long or hurt as deeply as it used to. I can now think more clearly, and am more easily able to begin navigating my way around it or through it. I am better now at seeing a less-than-positive exchange with someone from a more true perspective of what it is, and what it IS NOT. Oftentimes I will even dialogue out loud with the Universe, *OK, what is this about? What's going on here for me to see? What is in this for me—if anything?* The ego mind says, *They are obviously wrong,* and you are justified in holding the grudge. Spirit mind wants you to dig deeper.

I hope you can now see that relationship dilemmas really encapsulate all three principles. I need to figure out my PERSONAL RESPONSIBIL-ITY in this. I need to decide if I am ATTACHED to a certain belief about what the person said or did that probably has nothing to do with the other person. Is it me, who attached a judgment or a value based on my expectations to the act or the words of the other person? And thirdly, WHAT AM I BEING TAUGHT by this? What is being revealed to me, about me, and for me? *This* is the basis for learning and healing, and eliminating unnecessary drama and suffering for ourselves in regard to our relationships.

For whatever reason, this awareness and these practices do not come naturally. We have to consciously work to apply them. But the wonderful thing is that as we do the work, and as we are willing to see and willing to heal, it affects the quality of our relationships across the board. We do not have to begin anew with each person to work through the issues. As we bring a healed, whole version of ourselves to the table, things change. We are no longer dependent on anybody else to make us healed or whole. When you can disentangle from unhealthy relationship dynamics in this way, freedom and zen become part of your daily experience. It's beautiful!

I could probably write an entire book on each of these relationship principles. The point here, in *Zen in High Heels*, is to show you the deeper underlying truths of how relationships work so you may think differently about them. If you view your relationships through the lens of these spiritual principles, through a lens of inquisitiveness and desire for growth, you will see change. You will experience improvement: better, healthier relationships can be yours!

CHAPTER 12

Relationships Continued...

"Relationships don't last because of the good times, they last because the hard times were handled with love and care."

—ANMOL ANDORE

Taking personal responsibility, assuming a stance of non-attachment, and seeing difficult relationships as the opportunities for growth they are, does not always—does not even usually—turn a troublesome relationship spontaneously into a now positive or healthy one. Your healing work and new awareness will bring new communication and action toward others. If somehow things align and this opens them up to react differently in return, there is a possibility that you may evolve to an honest, healthy, vulnerable place together. Then we can celebrate! Healing! Victory! YES! YES! YES!

But many times, your new level of consciousness does not change the other person's half of the equation at all. They remain, for whatever reason, attached to the same level of awareness or lack of awareness and behavior. Your rise in awareness, however, will allow you to change your words and actions enough so you are able to disengage from the level where you are triggered. (This is the raising of your outlet metaphor.) You may have been going along your merry way, feeling fine, and WHAM! Whatever they said or did, or perhaps the way they said or did it, brought up a volcano of unpleasant emotion or sucked the air right out of your happy sail! Something flipped the switch, and all circuits went down. In this case, the circuits are: reasoning, rationale, and presence.

You being triggered means instead of acting, reacting, or speaking from the space of consciousness and personal awareness of the emotions that are being evoked, you simply fall back to default mode. You react instead how you used to react based on a previous belief or script that causes your ego to rear its head in your defense. Any actions that occur on your behalf from a place of being triggered, do not come from your higher Self. Ever. Your ego, however, will gladly cooperate with the forces of others to trip your trigger and subsequently distract you from your path. After all, you can justify your response, because he or she started it! It is not your fault they were a jerk.

Your healthy, authentic Self is able to remain UNtriggered by others, or at the very least, able to control any outward response from a triggered place. Your spiritual practices act as a generator, a backup to keep all systems running, despite the trigger.

As always, you only have control over you. If you need to leave a job or end a relationship, then do so. It is not at all uncommon to see how the person or relationship scenario you were in conflict with did its job (what your soul hired it to do), and your growth is no longer dependent on them being part of your life. No hard feelings. Your new boundaries are clear. Wish them well and keep moving forward.

Even if this is the case, if a relationship did not improve or heal, you have created a new frontier. For every time you interact with someone in a different, more honest, and conscious way, you raise the vibration of that moment. Depending where the other person is on their journey, and in that interaction, it may or may not be received in the spirit of your intention. And that is OK. If you come to the conversation or interaction with love and a desire to express yourself honestly, at the very least, you have been a gatekeeper for the possibility of a new and better connection. It may not yield an earthquake of change and healing, but you can quietly acknowledge within yourself your new competence about yourself, which will instill confidence to keep forging on this path of authenticity.

As we learned with acting in intention and integrity, you may walk away from certain relationships not just because of the other person, but because YOU are coming from a place of understanding and honoring YOU. You now realize that there is a lesson in every seemingly negative situation, even a blessing. Maybe learning what you do not want is the lesson. Thank you, Universe! Got it! I still may not have the answers for exactly what I do want, but you made that one crystal clear for me. I am certain that *THAT* is not what I want or need! With this realization, your personal zen factor just went up!

In the same regard, every situation that does open up or change and makes both you and the other person responsive in a new way, a way in which you both broaden your view and see each other's perspective is a success! And such success is worth every seeming failure you encounter along the way. Such success does not come about without you first stepping up with integrity and being brave enough to risk it. Risk being seen. Letting people see who you are is risky. But those relationships and experiences that thrive because of it will absolutely reward you with the sense of meaning and connection you've always longed for.

One of the benefits, or perhaps can even be stated as a repercussion of the awareness you gain in your growth, is that you can see, probably for the first time, how Unaware most other people are. When you lift the veil of unconsciousness from your eyes, it becomes so obvious who the others are who are still operating with limited, unconscious perception. Even others you have known for a very long time. You now see them, and their issues through your new, clearer eyes of consciousness.

This is the place of your new growth where you can very easily get sidetracked by focusing on "them." *If only they could see. If only I can help them see.* This is very, very common. I am here to warn you of this pitfall. It will feel like you have the very best of intentions. But mostly, this is your ego's attempt to distract you.

Your ego has been threatened. It senses that you are on a path to uncovering its restrictive, even destructive patterns in your life, and it seizes your beautiful, generous heart with a newfound diversion. If your ego mind can get you to focus on rescuing, or enlightening your unenlightened friend or family member, it will have succeeded in taking your mind off of your own journey! Your path stalls out. Your next step, or your next issue to tackle, gets shoved to the back. You are now fully committed to saving another. You have become attached to the idea of the outcome for them that you have experienced for yourself. You know this is possible, *if only* you could get them to see it! Beware of this trap. This is distraction disguised as care and concern.

We have all heard the saying, "Everybody is doing the best they can." This is really not an easily digested sentiment when we know people who could OBVIOUSLY be doing better. It is quite clear that many people could be making better decisions for themselves. What we're really meaning is this: everyone is being as conscious as they are ready to allow. If this is true, you may both drown if you try to "save" someone who is not ready, or not interested in being saved! You cannot want more for someone than they want for themselves. Give up thinking you know what's best for anyone else. Amen.

Oftentimes it is very easy to see recurring, undesired patterns when we look at other people. Have you ever noticed that people have their issues, and for the most part, someone's issues seem to be the same struggle, over and over again? People with money issues tend to have money issues their whole life, that is the theme. People who get cheated on, tend to get cheated on over and over. There's this "thing" that, until you do the work to really fix it, will just continue to reoccur and resurface. Sometimes in strange or less obvious ways, but the theme is the same. The Universe never tires of giving us recurring opportunities to experience the core issue. That is, until we heal it at the source of the original wounding that still lives deep inside of us.

If you feel you must offer some unsolicited advice or insight to someone in your close circle, do it once. Meditate on what you want to say and how you want to say it, so it is communicated with the intention of your heart. Just make it known that, "I am always here for you, don't hesitate to reach out," and, if appropriate, say, "I love you." Perhaps you pass along one of your most favorite, most helpful books. And then, here's the thing: That's it. That was your part. Period. It is NOT your role to worry, to follow up, or to give them yet another book. If they want a recommendation for a second book, they will ask you. Spending your energy thinking you know what is best for someone else's life path is undoubtedly a detriment to yours. An enlightened person does not try to convince others of anything. It does not work that way. When you are living a life on a path toward enlightenment, you do not attach to other people's journeys.

You make the best possible mentor by leading by example. I am certain that someone along your way will see in you something they would also like to have. It may come soon, or it may come later. But those people will inquire; they will ask you what you do. They will want to know how you improved your life. They will wonder how you remain so calm and unbothered amidst the chaos of the world. These are the people who are ready and willing recipients of your knowledge and your wisdom. This is with whom you share.

Forgiveness is another topic that can trip us up in relationships and on our path to inner peace. Needing to forgive can span across any type of relationship. I only want to touch on it briefly in case you feel unforgiveness is keeping you from growing on your spiritual path. If someone has done something absolutely horrible, immoral, or illegal to you—if you have been abandoned, betrayed, or physically or sexually abused ever in your life and you are not ready, willing, or able to forgive the person, I'm here to say THAT'S OK. Wait! Back it up! Did I just say unforgiveness is OK?

Any other spiritual growth book encourages, or counts forgiveness as essential, so what am I saying? What I am saying is that sometimes the violation was so egregious that your mind or your heart cannot jump from the place you are now—understandably wounded—to a place of "forgiveness." *Let bygones be bygones* is not applicable in this situation on this day. So feeling like that is what you must do can create a metaphorical concrete roadblock for you in other ways. I say, if you feel you cannot forgive the person or the circumstance that victimized you, then don't for now. Just allow yourself to work on all of the other principles for yourself. Work on understanding and healing yourself, and work on releasing all the ways the injustice holds you back or causes you to lash out.

I am suggesting instead of forgiveness in the sense of absolving the perpetrator for the pain they caused you, for now, work on not letting that event or that abuser have control over you TODAY. Don't let it control or hold you back today—be willing to look at the ways it might be. Your mind would love to keep you focused on the *could've* or the *should've* or the *WHY*. When you point the finger at someone in the past, it may very well be keeping you from assuming responsibility for today's growth and tomorrow's potential that is awaiting you.

Eventually, as you heal and grow on your path and rediscover your light and the love in you, you may take steps to forgive. Maybe never forgiving the person or people involved, but forgiving the Universe for the fact that it happened. Forgive yourself for any way you assumed blame for what happened. Sometimes we get caught up on the word "forgiveness." Maybe think of "forgive" in terms of acceptance. If not forgiveness, begin with *acceptance* of this reality—acceptance that these things did happen, and no matter how tightly you hold on to bitterness or blame, it will not change that fact.

Tend to your heart and tend to your spirit with compassion for what you've been through and with admiration for how you survived and how far you've come. No longer holding on to the darkness it instilled in you, but accepting that the current You grew stronger in many ways because of it. Don't dwell on the idea of forgiveness or the fact that you cannot forgive, or that you will NEVER forgive. It's OK—leave that declaration in your satchel perhaps for now, but do all of the other work that your life is calling you to do.

Your level of forgiveness or unforgiveness of a particular situation or person may need revisiting in the future, but today, let's accept and take the reins of healing in ways that are available to us. Despite any abuse, your truth of love and light remains your truth. I'm asking you to reclaim that! And know that any ways you have yet to forgive do not restrict you from pursuing your spiritual growth path. Embrace all of the other ways *Zen in High Heels* lays out for you to grow into everything you deserve to be!

We've addressed some difficult relationships and encounters with other people, but what about the relationships in your life that are not really particularly difficult or dramatic? Can we use spiritual principles to make these better, also? Say, for example, that you are in a committed relationship or marriage that is not necessarily tumultuous, but has you feeling unfulfilled or rather bored or stagnated. What do you do with this? There are many things you can do to try to improve this scenario. And guess what? They all begin with YOU.

So many women experience issues in their primary relationship, but refuse to bring it up to their partner! They gladly lament over the dull sense of anguish to their mother, or their best friend, but have yet to sit down to try to effectively communicate their honest feelings to their partner.

Many people say, *I do not want to have this conversation; I hate conflict!* We must reframe this! You experience conflict because there is something that needs to be resolved or better understood in the relationship. By definition, conflict in a relationship does not have to be a bad, horrible thing. Putting any issue(s) on the table via a conversation is the best, most direct chance of progress, growth, and elimination of the conflict! Plus, as you progress in your own spiritual practices, you will be better able to communicate what it is you feel and what it is you need, which is many times what has caused additional stumbling blocks when you may have tried to address conflict in your past. You are a better conflict resolver now! Initiating conflict resolution in a conversation is nothing to be afraid of anymore. It is simply a bridge to making things better.

If, despite your many requests to engage, your partner still does not plan any activities with you, but instead, plants him or herself in front of the TV every night after work, you can suggest couples therapy to find out what underlies this behavior. Suggest he or she get a physical. Get blood chemistry looked at to make sure there is not a biological reason they are withdrawn and tired.

Maybe you plan a change of scenery, a date night, or a weekend getaway. I know you want your partner to take initiative and do this, but they are not. So do you stew and pout about this, or live in the reality of what IS? Decide your intention of having fun with your spouse, and do what you can do to make this happen.

If you suggest couples therapy, in the safety of a counseling setting, you may discover that you did not sufficiently communicate your desires, or maybe you were not able to adequately communicate the feelings behind your desires for your partner to truly understand what it is you are desiring to change. I've talked to so many women who consider it too risky, women who just *know* that they will get shot down and defeated in their attempt to suggest counseling to their partner. But you may be surprised! Maybe they have been unhappy as well, unsure of how to address their concerns.

As we learned earlier, growth may occur in the extra space of possibility. It is crucial to be open to the possibility of your partner agreeing to therapy. Perhaps their mind is not as closed as you believe it to be. If you make the suggestion, but you were correct and your partner is not interested in couples therapy, I suggest YOU go to therapy. Have a safe place to vent and to understand the root of your discontent better. Just because they choose not to go does not mean you cannot go. You get to make that decision for yourself. If you are willing to look for it in any circumstance, you will always find somewhere, to some degree, you have a choice.

Perhaps your partner has never been particularly social, but you thought you could change them? Look at your own life and free time, and add an activity you would enjoy, a charity organization, a book club, or a sports team, and you get more engaged. Figure out ways you can get your social engagement and social stimulation, so that perhaps you can return home, more filled up and more appreciative of the comfort and safety that your homebody partner provides you.

There are always initial actions that you can take on behalf of the couplehood to improve it. Try as many as you need to, of course backed by the right attitude and intention, and watch things change. The relationship has a chance to bloom if you do something different than you have been doing. Your life has a chance to blossom if you give yourself permission to meet some of your own needs, turning then to your partner for the strengths they add to your relationship and to your life. The strengths that may have gotten lost in the routine or rut that has become your day-to-day existence.

Not all relationships can survive an attempt to change the dynamic, but many can. If we think in terms of that soul contract, what you're doing, in essence, is trying to renegotiate the terms. Renegotiation of a contract requires the agreement of both parties. This does not change the fact that the solution begins with you. Stop waiting on the other person. Be clear about what is bothering you, or what need you feel is not being met in the partnership. Follow that up with taking action by having the conversation to see what difference your forthright communication makes.

Look at the relationships of your life with new eyes. Become an observer. Listen to others! You will be fascinated by your discoveries!

Do it! Do the work! This kind of spiritual work is tremendously reward-ing. From a place of healing and understanding, we are then able to carry our own weight and function in relationships that are free and healthy: reciprocative, nurturing relationships that edify us.

Put whatever situation you are desiring change through the follow-ing questions:

- Who am I?
- What is my intention?
- What is my intention in this situation?
- How does this make me feel?
- Where does this stem from? When have I felt similarly before?
- What variables do I have control over?
- What am I grateful for?

If you do not see clear action or solution, keep the troublesome rela-tionship in your prayers, in your meditation space, and then give it some time to breathe. Detach from it needing to resolve in this moment, if it is not. In the meantime, choose to be at peace with what IS. In other words, you are working toward resolution, but not wasting time worrying until that happens. Focus instead for a while on other areas of your life or people in your life you can tend to. Can you shift your attention to a different co-worker or family member who is not causing you trouble? Who can you write a thank you note to today? What other aspects of personal growth can you put your attention on today?

Set an example for yourself; send a message to the Universe. You are willing to be a good steward; you are willing to apply yourself and take advantage of opportunities you do have. Show your monkey mind that although you have some concerns about the state of your primary relationship, you are actually the one in control and you are choosing to be grateful today, and to focus on the things you are able to do something about today. Then circle back around to the relationship in question.

Personal Responsibility, assuming responsibility for what you can do something about, Non-attachment, choosing to be in your own peace or joy despite the actions of another, and Relationships as teachers, seeking the lesson for yourself—all of these principles apply the same in the somewhat challenging relationships as they do in the super challenging ones. I am excited for you to implement these new tools in your life!

PART IV

Tending to Your Vessel

CHAPTER 13

Love Your Body

"I said to my body softly, 'I want to be your friend.' It took a long breath and replied, "I have been waiting my whole life for this."

—NAYYIRAH WAHEED

As much as we established meditation as a fundamental thread throughout the tapestry of our evolution, in the broader picture, so too can we count relationships as a primary component of our growth. We explored the relationship with our deeper Self and our relationships with others. It is now time to address your relationship with the vessel for your soul: your physical body.

Oftentimes in spiritual conversations, in the realm of spiritual teachings, our body is not mentioned, or it is merely glossed over. How we feel about and how we care for or neglect our body is a significant part of our life journey. This relationship too, has things to teach us. If you will allow it, your spiritual journey and your physical fitness journey can be intimately connected: each impacting and supporting the other.

When you are plugged in and tending to your spiritual work, you will feel stronger in who you are. You will feel more calm, you will be able to let the little annoyances in life roll off your back. Likewise, when you are tending to your physical body through fitness and nutrition and general well-being practices, you will feel strong in who you are. You will feel more calm and more able to let little annoyances in life roll off your back!

I could say what you might expect a spiritual growth book to say: *It's what's on the inside that counts. Put no importance on external standards of what you look like. Beauty is fleeting.* But it is more honest to acknowledge that how we look and how we feel, in terms of having health and having energy, are of absolute significance in our life journey. Now it is true, I am not speaking of particular measurements, a certain weight, certain breast size, or hair length. But I am saying that physically being the best that you can be, that caring for and tending to your physical body, which includes exercise and eating right, will support you in how you are able to show up in the world. Good health allows you to show up for your life and not just sit on the sidelines watching while others engage.

Attention to your physical body and its needs is a way for you to honor the deeper, truer spiritual part of your Self. So although this is not a book on how to get in shape or lose weight, as you grow on your spiritual path, you will make better decisions across the board for yourself and for your life. This should include better decision making for your physical health. Actively pursuing physical health and fitness will teach you things you need to know for your journey of personal growth.

Unfortunately, the intimate relationship we have with our physical body is a primary relationship with which many of us struggle. We are bombarded with images through social media and advertisers of what it means to be fit and beautiful. We are constantly reminded by these often photoshopped and filtered images that the way we are is not enough. We are not quite right. We could be better. There is pressure, and false hope promised in this piece of exercise equipment, this pill or that cream. Maybe lipo those love handles, or surgically insert these implants...then, you *might* have a chance to feel like you are enough! Maybe then you will feel like you are worthy of the good things that life has to offer.

Back when we were talking about the inner voice, that *roommate* in our minds that will not shut up, part of the excessive, obsessive chatter, especially as women, is in regard to our physical body. That part of our mind seems to have enormous commentary about our physical appearance. It blabs about things we cannot control, *You are too short.* And things we should be able to control, *You are too fat.*

You may have noticed this when you started observing your thoughts: many of the negative ones are indeed directed at the image you see in the mirror. Just as we had to become familiar with and friends with our deeper selves, now too, we must become familiar with and friends with our body. Every single time you notice a negative thought directed at your body, *I hate my thighs*, *My arms look HUGE in this top*, whatever it is, you must practice replacing that thought immediately with a statement of gratitude. *Thank you, body. So grateful I have the mobility of both of my legs! So grateful my arms work to hold and play with my pet or my child*! Start there, begin making general gratitude statements about the functions of your body. Then add in actual body parts you visually appreciate. *I do love my* _____.

Be vigilant of your thoughts. When the ego mind wants to compare you with others, remember there is probably always going to be someone out there with a better booty or better abs. But guess what—there are lots of people out there who would love to have your booty or your waistline! Get over comparing, unless you are using that in a positive and aspirational way as inspiration to make better choices for yourself. As with every other chapter, every other principle, keep the focus where it belongs: on YOU.

As author Louise Hay said, "You have been criticizing yourself for years and it hasn't worked. Try approving yourself and see what happens!"

When you take care of your physical self, you will become less obsessed by the desire to meet external expectations; rather you will be free to feel good and enjoy the benefits of the improved health that you will have earned. You will appreciate your strengths which you will find exponentially outnumber any flaws. You will experience the freedom of being and accepting YOU. You will discover how improving this core relationship will contribute to your ability to experience zen. Taking care of yourself enables you to exude not only physical beauty, but also inner beauty, and an energetic vitality that will all be felt and experienced by any others who are fortunate enough to come into your presence!

Deciding your physical health is important, and worthy of your attention is a noble investment—one that pays dividends in so many ways: the way you look, the way you feel, the way you think, the way you sleep. Making time in your schedule to exercise and prepare healthier food is not vain or selfish! I can hear some of you now; *I am so busy tending to everyone else in my life, like my family and my boss, that I don't have time to exercise or prepare healthy meals. I cannot take time away from my obligations to others who need me.*

Caring for others at the expense of your own health and energy ends up a losing game for everyone involved. When you are exhausted and sick, you are of no use to anyone, including yourself. All the work you do on yourself, for your Self, spiritually, emotionally and/ or physically only allows you to show up better! Like they say on the airplane, *put the oxygen mask on YOU FIRST, then assist your child, or whoever else may need your assistance.* When your cup is full, you have so much more to offer the other people in your life! You have so much more to offer the world. A well cared for You has so much to offer those people who need you! It's all related and intertwined. All the things we seek begin with knowing, understanding and honoring ourselves. This includes honoring our physical needs. This allows us the best chance to live a life fulfilling our purpose.

If and when you tend to the needs of your body in the ways it was designed to be cared for, you will grow to appreciate it. You will be grateful for it, and you will be amazed by what it offers you in return. Giving your body adequate exercise, rest and nutrition will yield external results as a by-product of your care. You will probably slim down, tone up, have more energy, your eyes will brighten, your skin may glow. This will increase your happiness with what you see in the mirror. Regardless of the number on the scale, you will be able to smile and be grateful for how the journey of physical fitness allows your strength and your self-confidence to shine.

Physical fitness is a $100 billion business! We are undeniably searching for answers, or THE answer to finally solve our body image woes. In *Zen in High Heels,* I am saying we can use physical fitness, specifically exercise, as yet another tool in our toolbox for life. Exercise is a profound tool for spiritual and personal evolution. You will come to see, if you are not already aware, that deep at the core, in addition to your physical body, most attempts to improve your physical fitness will also engage and challenge your mind and spirit. Because of this truth, we can use testing and improving our physical fitness as a gateway to the soul.

The parallels and the metaphors your physical health journey give you that directly relate to your spiritual journey will become obvious. As you gain outward measurable strength, you will discover untapped inner strength. You will then be able to really enjoy what we discussed in the very beginning of the book: your high heels and that perfect fitting pair of jeans! They will be icing on the cake, accessories to your healthy and fit zen-filled self—not merely items of attachment that we think will somehow give our lives meaning and make us worthy of love or validation from others.

If you do not feel good about yourself, putting your focus on physical fitness is probably the quickest way to change that. Exercise induces positive chemical changes in both your body and your brain. It serves as an easily measurable sense of accomplishment. Getting a degree, raising well-rounded children, and building your retirement fund may all contribute to making you feel secure and "good" about yourself, but these take many years to achieve. Fitness accomplishments can be achieved much more quickly. Can't do ten push-ups today? Work on it every other day and at the end of 30 days, I bet you can! And when you do accomplish this goal, you will know it was YOU who did it! No one else did the push-ups for you! There you go; now you feel stronger. You are stronger.

Consistent exercise is a surefire way of raising your self-esteem, your self-respect and your self-confidence. Increased self-esteem, self-respect and self-confidence can't help but positively affect other areas of your life. Bring an improved, stronger, healthier version of you to your interactions with others, to your job, your partner, to your children, and watch your life improve! You will feel better; your life will feel better.

Your body is designed to perform. We get better and thrive when we challenge it beyond its comfort zone. You can choose not to explore this, perhaps label yourself as a nonathlete, and in doing so, leave so much of your potential on the table. If you are putting out the call to your life to expand, to live confidently in your own personal strength—whatever your age—physical fitness must be part of the equation. Exercise must be a fundamental, non-negotiable part of your journey.

I've heard many women claim they do not consider themselves an athlete. Well, you are. It is not accurate to say you are a nonathlete. It is more accurate to say that's not who you have been up until now. Or if you claim you *used to be* an athlete back in the day, perhaps you have just not engaged your inner athlete in a while! Your body is designed the same as an athlete's body. I've heard women claim they are certainly not an endurance athlete. Well, again, you are. Life is the longest endurance event there is! If you are over 20, or 30 or 40 or 50...you have a track record of surviving, of enduring! Put your body through half of what your mind and spirit have already been through—endurance is unarguably part of your constitution. You're practically a SuperHero! You can doubt it, or you can tap into it! I challenge you to be your own SuperHero!

If you choose to get moving, you will see that your athleticism was just lying dormant, waiting for you to activate it. There are so many inspiring stories of people who were couch potatoes with a myriad of health issues, who then made the decision, one step at a time, one dumbbell at a time, one yoga class at a time to change their lives, and they did. As a bonus, each of these people found more than their muscles, or more than their stamina. They found an inner part of them that is stronger than they knew. They found resilience. They found discipline. And ultimately, they found freedom!

If you do have a disability, an injury, or any actual bodily limitations, this principle still applies to you. You are free to argue all the reasons you "can't"—or you can figure out what it is you are able to do, and work from there. Again, just like spiritual growth, CHALLENGING YOURSELF FROM THE LEVEL WHERE YOU ARE TODAY IS THE KEY.

The experiences in life that challenge us and do not feel easy to get through, give us opportunity to emotionally and spiritually grow stronger and better. So, too, does the body grow stronger and better by being challenged with activities that do not feel easy to do. The metaphors, if you should choose this path of physical health and fitness will astound you. It is a beautiful parallel, the physical and the spiritual journey. Let's take a deeper look at how this is so.

Ask anyone who has trained for their first marathon. They learned the meaning behind the term "blood, sweat and tears." Was their training a physical journey? Yes, of course. Was it a mental journey? Even more so. Did it at some point become spiritual? For sure. Negotiating, even pleading somewhere along the way with all three: the body, the mind, and the Universe itself!

Showing up to the gym or for the workout easily serves as a metaphor for showing up for your life. Something is about to require your participation, and you are present for roll call. Just as no one else can live your life for you, no one else can exercise for you. No matter what anyone else is doing, you get to decide if today is a day you will show up for YOU.

If you haven't been one to enjoy exercise up until this point, and you consider it an arduous task, reframe it as an opportunity. Your exercise time is the opportunity for you to get in touch with your body. Verbalize your intention to your body: I am here to support you, to honor you, and to connect with you during this hour (or whatever the time frame).

Despite whatever else is going on in your life, you send a message to your body via your workout time that it matters to you. *You are important enough for me to devote some time and energy specifically to you.* Utilize previously learned principles: set an intention, and be grateful. There are a million things your body allows you to do to be grateful for, including this workout in front of you!

Increasing your physical fitness level will require you, at some point, to face your demons. Demons, meaning any perceived limits or weakness you have been carrying around as part of you. Demons, meaning the resistance you feel as you try to push past those previously perceived limits. If you refuse to hide or lie to yourself anymore by acknowledging those limitations that are usually self-imposed, come face-to-face with those demons but don't back down, make the effort to push through them, you will earn satisfaction and self-confidence. An undeniably improved relationship with your body will emerge.

We find it is precisely in the moment we are putting in the effort, challenging ourselves beyond our current comfort level, or perceived capacity, that we usually experience those demons, the parameters that the mind would have us believe are fixed and true. *Here*, it will say, *is your limit!* When you find yourself on the hill—literally or meta-phorically—your weaknesses, those inner beliefs about yourself are revealed. And they are revealed in the most intimate, undeniable way, right there inside your own head. Now what? What are you going to tell yourself now that it's not easy? Even more importantly, what are you going to *do*? Will you try? Will you quit?

Maybe you even hear the faint or not-so-faint voices of others from your past. The parent who said you'll never amount to anything, the kids on the playground who picked you last to be on their team, the coach who called you clumsy, the sister or brother who said you are lazy. If you are going to conquer this hill, or this obstacle in front of you, you must challenge those voices. Make those voices your train-ing partner if you can! You must prove them wrong. Even one more step, or one more minute—anything that is beyond the initial whine of the weaker part of your mind crying that you must quit, is prog-ress. It is actually powerful progress. Just as with the other spiritual principles we have covered, *any* time you open yourself up to the possibility of things being different, you create space for a better outcome. Growth occurs in the unrestricted space of possibility—outside of current or past confines.

Keep digging and digging, and just like your emotional and spiritual work, if you dig deep enough, challenge yourself enough and re-negotiate terms with your internal dialogue, if you will honor your body for its potential, without your pre-imposed restrictions, you will find truth. Truth lies at the core of training. All is well. Endorphins flow and you gain satisfaction unlike ANY material possession or outside source can give you.

A physical challenge, or an actual hill during your workout provides the opportunity to unveil your mental fortitude, or lack of mental fortitude. It's just You and this hill. The hill is not going anywhere. The hill is not moving. What are you going to do? Who will you be in this moment? How will you show up? The hill can serve as a metaphor in your life. What does it represent for you today? What challenge or person in your life does the hill represent? And then observe, Who are you when things are not easy? Who are you in this workout moment, and in your life in non-workout moments when you are confronted with the need to dig deeper? Do you tend to give up? Give in? Put it off until next time? Personal revelations are especially highlighted in moments we feel challenged when no one else is around. Who is going to know if you put this off until tomorrow? If you quit today just shy of your goal? This is where you build or chip away at integrity where it matters most: WITH YOUR SELF.

A workout challenge becomes easy access to the deeper, truer You because the hill is not the least bit impressed with your status in society. It is not going to ask you what kind of car you drive or how much money you have. The hill doesn't care if you are unemployed, or if you have legal issues. It does not care one bit how much you weigh or what brand your sneakers are. The hill does not care if you played a sport in high school, or what you did yesterday. The hill is there to ask you one simple question. Who are you right now, in *this* moment?

Tackling the hill requires presence. Interesting. We thought this was a discussion about physically hiking or running or biking up a hill, only to realize that the hill made us present with ourselves in this moment. The hill wants to know who we are on the inside right now. Presence is a major spiritual principle, and what do you know, we are finding it through a physical challenge.

As with any attempt to grow in any way, your mind, in response to the challenge of the hill, may have gone bonkers! Resistance shows up, alerting you that this is a new, perhaps undoable, unsafe and certainly unnecessary task. *Give up,* it shouts! But now we can go back to what we learned in meditation. These are just thoughts, not necessarily true thoughts. You get to decide. You get to allow a moment of space before you decide to give in. Challenge those thoughts. See what you are made of. More often than not, you will be pleasantly surprised!

Turns out the challenge right in front of you serves as a physical, tangible experience creating a window to much deeper meaning than getting to the top of this hill. It is just You and the challenge that is presenting itself to you. That's what it comes down to, period. As in life outside of your workouts, in difficult moments, you get to decide how you will show up. You get to decide if you will remain in your comfort zone, or if today is the day to explore and push the boundaries.

Can you see the connection? The pursuit of physical fitness is also a journey of self-discovery. It is in challenging the natural desire to take the easy route and in the pursuing of more for yourself that you are able to revise your relationship with Resistance. You begin to recognize that initial old, familiar pushback, the one Steven Pressfield calls resistance with a capital R–as a necessary part of the journey. It is the same voice of opposition we experienced as we attempted to grow in other ways. But we already learned in our work of the earlier chapters, Resistance is not something to be afraid of, but rather something to acknowledge its presence and with grateful determination, and with all due respect, TAKE IT DOWN.

If you have found that Resistance is a domineering player in your search for emotional and spiritual growth, conquering it here in physical training may be just what you need to begin navigating through it and past it in other areas. Conquer Resistance here, show yourself what you are made of, and somehow Resistance or internal pushback does not feel as scary when it appears in other areas of your life!

When you get intentional about seeking better health and fitness for yourself, when you get curious about and committed to exploring your capabilities, you'll find practices that work for you. You will find practices that support a healthier version of you. This exploration will allow you to break through and eliminate some of the barriers that have been inhibiting you in your desire to reach your physical potential.

Deepak has a saying, "Resist this thing, and you resist the whole Universe." I often think of that when I encounter a hill on my runs. *I could resist this hill. Part of me feels like giving in and walking it, or taking another route.* But I realize with this Deepak quote, if I resist this challenge before me, I also forgo the pot of gold it may yield on the other side of it. Or contrarily, I can send a message to the Universe by attacking the hill, *Go ahead and put challenges in front of me; I will not give up. I will tackle this challenge and show you that I am determined. I will persevere in finding my strength. I will persevere in my seeking of truth!* I do not resist the hill. I do not resist the whole Universe. And I learn by working hard and enduring that my body becomes stronger. I become stronger and more capable of tackling the next hill. These are the traits I want in my life, not just in my workouts. I want to be determined; I want to persevere; I want to be strong! *Thank you, hill, for the gift of discovery you provided me today. Thank you, hill, for the chance to practice being who I want to be today: determined and strong, not a quitter!*

I use the hill as one example of a daunting challenge that your work-out may dangle as a carrot outside your current level of fitness. It may not be an actual hill. For some, the "hill" shows itself as the alarm clock. Just getting yourself up for the workout that is waiting may be your daunting challenge. Do you hit SNOOZE, SNOOZE and SNOOZE?—putting it off again until tomorrow? Or do you break through that desire for a few extra minutes of comfort, and show the weaker part of you that things are going to change? Conscious You is now in charge! If the snooze button is your metaphorical hill, and now you realize that, make adjustments to your nighttime routine to support the morning routine you aspire to.

Try different things. Be curious about yourself and what works for you. For the longest time, I proclaimed that spin class was not for me! I tried it once; I did not enjoy it AT ALL! I was so uncomfortable! The seat was too hard, and my thighs rubbed it; my butt bones hurt. Anyway, cut to many years later—I wanted to support a friend of mine who was opening his own spin studio—so I went. Same uncomfortable experience, so I said, *I wish you all the luck, but spinning is just not for me!* To which he promptly suggested that I needed specific bike shorts. So, despite the first time putting the bike shorts on feeling like I was wearing a diaper, I tried spin class with shorts made specifically for that activity, and now it's something I enjoy regularly! I enjoy myself a good spin class! In my padded bike shorts, my butt doesn't hurt at all! And spin class strengthens my legs and glutes in a different way than running. It's a great complementary activity. Lesson learned—don't force yourself to do something that you hate doing, but also be open to the possibility that as you get more fit, or as technology changes, you may indeed grow to like an activity that you previously banned from your list of fun activities for fitness.

If you choose to participate in a physical activity or sport that requires a skill that you don't already have—you take up tennis, for example—you can smile as you gain confidence seeing how much you improve with practice over time. Not unlike the spiritual principles, practice even when it doesn't come naturally to you, and be in awe as you find yourself becoming more skilled. Meditation, when consistently practiced, does get easier. Pausing before reacting in a triggering moment is not at first an easy thing to do, but the more you do it, the more natural it becomes. What you once found difficult—the tennis serve—you now find much more of the time, you are getting the ball to the other side of the net AND in the lines where you want it! Beautiful analogy: sport and spirituality. Practice enables growth.

In your meditation time, seek to identify your deeper intention behind being physically fit. Understanding your *why* by establishing your intention will surely impact your decision not to hit snooze, but rather to show up! Hmm, we gain progress spiritually and emotionally by clarifying our intentions. And now we see intention can also play a role in physical fitness progress!

Just like other growth principles, there is no shortcut, no app for this. It is You and You. It's You versus You. You supporting You. When you do conquer obstacles like the alarm clock or the hill, you gain an intrinsic satisfaction. You have a victory to claim for yourself on that day. You gain momentum. Furthermore, when you accomplish this bigger thing that you thought you could not do, that seemed almost impossible: the first spin class, the 10K, the marathon, the triathlon, hiking the Himalayas, it cannot help but make you wonder, *What else did I think was impossible in my life that might actually be possible?*

ZEN IN HIGH HEELS

Physical training can be a catalyst to seeking other positive changes in your life because it is not just your body that is activated, but your mind and spirit as well!

This is not to say to find your zen you must train your body for an Ironman event. Find something that challenges YOU. Improving physical fitness, like every other spiritual growth principle, is always possible starting from exactly where you are in this moment. Maybe you just want to touch your toes! Maybe it is a 5K, a dance class, or learning to box or play pickleball. Maybe showing up consistently to that yoga class is the thing you need to be doing. There are too many options to list. Find something you are not currently doing, that you would like to do, but that you are not sure you can do, and do THAT. It is in the keeping of your commitment to yourself; it is in the trying and in the expanding of your Self that you gain fitness and that you break through and grow in additional meaningful ways.

Although you may not desire to achieve a massively challenging physical feat, it is still beneficial and of utmost importance to move your body most days. You will feel better. Exercise can decrease the symptoms and decrease the amount of medication needed for almost all medical conditions you can name. If you are just getting started, talk with your doctor first, but also, do research on your own. Find books, articles and stories about others who have used exercise and an active lifestyle to turn their life around! Instead of watching 30 minutes of funny cats on TikTok, search YouTube for fitness success stories or motivational teachers. Get inspired by what has been achieved by others, and become aware of ways you may be hindering yourself with a belief of what is or is not possible for you.

Additionally, exercise helps release pent-up energy that might otherwise show up mentally and physically as anxiety, low mood, ulcers, etc. Regular exercise will help you better manage the stress in your life. Stress and frustrations in life build a particularly heavy, negative energy in us. And at times when your life feels unruly and out of control, showing up for the workout creates a sense of structure and stability—something you can count on yourself for. No matter what else goes wrong, or what else you cannot control today, you get to decide if you exercise today or not.

I have found during difficult times, my ability to get through the day versus feeling barely able to survive it, is closely linked to my physical activity that day. My body absolutely carried me through the hardest times of my marital separation and divorce. I was so numb and so confused and so broken. The only thing I could make a choice about some days that made sense to me was to work out. I tried many times on the treadmill to outrun what felt like clouds of darkness descending on me. I was attempting to outrun whatever was causing the downward spiral of my thoughts. The negative ego mind was running a strong repeating loop, *You are too tired to work out. You are too stressed to work out today. What's the use? You may not survive this emotional/life blow; let's worry about that, and about all the other things that might happen.* NO, ego mind, for the next 30–60 minutes, take a back seat. I am working out. I am going to breathe hard, change my chemistry, get stronger, and remind myself that *I WILL SURVIVE!*

So many things were out of my control. Working out felt like a deposit I could make toward a better future. I would crank up my favorite playlist and drown out the inner voice of negativity and despair, if only for the hour in the gym.

Here's the thing. Maybe it did not make me feel GREAT, but it always made me feel a little bit better. Maybe working out did not completely rid my mind of the negativity, I may not have completely wiped out the feelings of despair. But what I did do, was send a message to those suckers: *I'm not going down easily! I'm not giving in to you. You have met a worthy adversary and I will be back again tomorrow, continuing my effort to wipe you out, one workout at a time!*

Here was a chance to practice what I had been learning in other areas of my life. I can have a negative thought, but it is not who I am. The negative thought does not necessarily own me, or identify me just because it is there! Awareness of this truth gives me the opportunity to choose how I will move forward. Will I express it, or attach to it, or just acknowledge it and still continue to choose a positive behavior for myself in that moment? This is another practical example of spiritual principles in action. I had the awareness now, and also the tool to claim my own power in the situation.

When I had made a decision to honor myself with a workout, I was then better able to get through that day. I began thanking my body for supporting me. *Thank you* I would say after each workout. I still do that today! Genuinely feeling grateful for its contribution to my life has deepened my connection with my body. I honor this vessel that carried me through. I listen to her more; I pay attention to signals she sends me. I realized she wanted to go to bed earlier. And so I did, for which she rewarded me in the morning with more energy and mental clarity.

It was the beginning of what continues to be a beautiful, reciprocal primary relationship of my life. I give her what she needs to function optimally and she rewards me in innumerable ways throughout each day. I cherish her. It turned out that even though there were other people involved in the stressful and painful circumstances I was experiencing, getting through the most difficult time of my life began with ME getting right with ME. This resulted in a cascade of outward circumstances getting better. Isn't that ironic? Not really. It is another parallel between spiritual and physical growth—as we have said all along, change starts with YOU. You get right with You and watch your life turn around.

I am still a work in progress, I get off track or overscheduled, or eat less healthy when I travel, but at least now I know how to get back on track. I know what "back on track" looks and feels like for me. I have tried different foods, amounts of exercise, amounts of sleep to know how my body functions best. This knowledge is invaluable! This sacred understanding of how *my* body works best is a direct result of my effort and willingness to listen. Again, exactly as it is with spiritual growth. There is a willingness to listen (meditate) and put forth effort based on what is revealed for me, and I see positive results! I love the parallels!

Before my quest for more wellness and vitality, I would just let the tides of circumstance determine if I worked out or how I ate. Now I can be much more conscious, more proactive, and strive for better choices more often. And just like I can veer off track spiritually, but not as far, or not as often, because I am equipped with tools and I understand how my mind and how the Universe work together, I may veer off track with my fitness or nutrition, but I have a much clearer understanding of even the smallest ways to get back on track. I now know what physical wellness feels like for myself, which allows me to be more aware of when I am not functioning optimally.

Just as with spiritual growth, when you establish for yourself what the physical part of you needs in order to thrive and you honor that with the choices you make, you gain integrity with your Self. No one, and no circumstance, can take that integrity from you; you earned it. This is how you gain the confidence to keep pressing forward on your path, despite the voice of Resistance or other naysayers in your life! This is a building block for all the many ways you want to show up and shine in your life! I would not exchange the confidence I experience from being fit and taking care of myself for *any* car, any amount of Instagram followers, or any amount of material abundance. It is priceless.

Figure out all the ways you can care for and nurture your Self, and watch as the Universe supports your effort. You will find that this, too, translates outside of the workout realm. If you are respectful and honoring of your physical self, it is far less likely you will tolerate a relationship with anyone else who is not honoring you. Contrarily, if you mistreat and ignore your needs, it is almost impossible to notice when another is mistreating or ignoring your needs also. Your commitment to yourself, or lack of commitment, is the gauge that feels "normal" on how you should expect to be treated.

Fitness, like the other principles, is not a fixed equation. There is not a one-exercise-fits-all approach. It can be a combination of so many athletic pursuits: boxing, basketball, weight training, Zumba, Pilates, running, or yoga. All or a combination of these activities can get you fit. It is commonly accepted that there are four pillars that create optimal physical fitness: cardiovascular fitness, flexibility, strength and balance or core stability. Seek fun and challenging ways to improve all of these areas for yourself. In addition to the feel-good chemicals exercise releases, exercise can also serve mental health by being a wonderful social outlet. Join a running club, a tennis league, go to a ballroom dance studio. Becoming part of a group centered around a physical activity can help you stay accountable and help you meet like-minded people. Exercise is a win-win-win choice!

If you are on an honest journey of self-discovery, there are things you will learn about yourself during your workout time that you will not learn during meditation, or by reading a book, or by attending a seminar. Interesting, fascinating things about you. You will come in contact with limits you thought were there, and limits you did not know were there. You will learn the power of your mind. You will learn that the benefits of physical fitness have very little to do with a number on the scale. You will discover what is true for you: you can either lift the ten-pound dumbbell, or you cannot. You can either run a mile without stopping, or you cannot. It does no good to judge. No more of *I should be this, or I shouldn't be that.* Just move from the reality of where you are. There really is no judgment around it. It is what it is. Where are you stronger than you believed? Where are you fooling yourself, and you are actually weaker than you believed?

With this knowledge, you can then put your attention and focus towards working on your life from the truth of where you are. This is the truth then become a platform for jumping and moving forward on your path. Make choices that will make today and tomorrow a better reality for you. The value of physical activity on your spiritual path is that it gives you a chance to not just THINK about ways you want to conquer your sabotaging mind, or even SAY out loud ways you plan to conquer your sabotaging, limiting mind, but to actually demonstrate to the limited version of you, to the Resistance and to the Universe that you are determined in ways big or small to challenge it! Fear may rear its head, but fear is no longer the dictator of your behavior—in or out of the gym!

CHAPTER 14

Nourish and Nurture

"Enjoy the journey as you strive for wellness."

—LAURETTE GAGNON BEAULIEU

*W*e cannot talk about care of our physical vessel without consideration of how we fuel it. There are what seems like a million diets: paleo, Mediterranean, Gluten-free, Vegan, Keto, Vegetarian, Low-carb, No-carb, the blood-type diet, etc. The daily choices we make in regard to the food we eat do play a role in how we fit into our jeans, but more importantly, in how we feel. Food affects our mood. Food affects our chemistry. Food affects our energy or lack of it. The wrong food can feed or flare conditions like diabetes, inflammation, and obesity.

I am not a nutritionist. I am someone who has scoured books on nutrition and listened to experts via podcasts for years. I have used trial and error to find my way as an aging athlete and find my way to better vitality. I've tried to clean up my diet over the years, very specifically for health reasons. I used to get sick all the time, catching every cold that was going around. I would joke, *Don't call me if you are sick, because I will probably catch it over the phone!* It was ridiculous. I exercised, didn't smoke, had medium stress, but I was obviously doing something wrong!

As I delved deeper into what foods and supplements support immunity, I started learning about alkalizing. This made me eat more green things. I learned about juicing, which helped me incorporate more fruits and vegetables. I cut back on dairy. And, it helped. Instead of ridding myself of junk food overnight, and instead of demonizing or completely cutting out specific foods, I used the idea of adding more of what I wanted and needed. Eventually, my cravings and taste changed; yours will too.

Like all other aspects of this book, I do not claim to have the exact answer for you. What I have found works for me might not work for you. I cannot recommend a specific diet plan for you. I can't advise you what to eat, how much to eat or what time to eat. But I can encourage you with the idea that you can determine what is right for yourself. If what you are doing is not working, research other ways and try other things. I can encourage you that small, incremental changes are probably the way to go (unless you are facing a true health crisis that would call for a complete overhaul).

Oftentimes the root of overeating, or indulging in things like excessive sugar or excessive alcohol, stems from emotional stress and/
or emotional issues we are trying to bury or avoid dealing with. I've
heard the saying in regard to weight issues, *It's not what you're eating;
it's what is eating you.* As part of a wellness process of doing the work
of the earlier chapters, you will probably be addressing, healing, and
possibly eliminating these deeper nudges to distract yourself and
numb yourself out with such excess. The spiritual work gives you
some of the things that overeating or overdrinking subconsciously
seek to fill. As you experience new levels of inner peace, and a less
shakable, truer version of you, you will find that you look for lifestyle
choices that support this improved version of you, which will include
moderation, not excess. You will desire to take care of your body.

Chris Powell, trainer and creator of the *EXTREME WEIGHT LOSS* television show, once said that when he first sees his obese clients, he
does not see the extra 100 or 200 pounds they are carrying; instead,
what he sees are 100 or 200 broken promises. He has found that at
the core of excessive weight gain are all the times a person promised
themselves to start but did not follow through. Or all the times they
gave up, and gave in to the voices, the excuses, to the weaker part of
themselves. They felt the Resistance, and gave into it.

We are such creatures of habit. Because we are creatures of habit,
it feels overwhelming to think, *I need to get from A to Z.* It feels overwhelming when I consider taking away something that I believe gives
me comfort today with the thought that it might someday pay off
somewhere in the distant future!

What does feel good, is taking the reins and working on one element at a time to improve. Drink more water. Don't eat past 8:00 p.m. Use coconut creamer instead of dairy creamer. Add a handful of spinach or kale to your smoothie (you won't even taste it!). Small ways that you listen to your body and care for yourself build that intrinsic sense of confidence and motivation to continue.

As with ALL the practices in *Zen in High Heels*, find the nutrition habits that work FOR YOU. I could tell you exactly what I do and exactly how I do it, but if you followed my plan to a T, you would not have the exact same result. Your chemistry is different from mine, your genes and heredity are different from mine, your lifestyle is different than mine. Keeping a food journal helps you stay on track? Do that! Joining a support group or food system like Jenny Craig helps keep you accountable? Do that! Tracking and counting your steps lights a fire to be more active? Do that! Try different vegetables, try different fruits, see which ones you enjoy and which ones satiate you. Eat more of those! If fasting for 24 hours on occasion makes you feel good, do that! If intermittent fasting within a 24 hour period makes you feel good and energized, by all means, DO THAT!

If you enjoy cooking, learn healthier alternatives to some of your favorites. You never know—you may actually like the healthier alternative ingredient or find the alternative way of preparing your food tastes as good, or even better to you! And, like all the principles teach: you have choices! You get to decide. It takes a willingness to pay attention, and notice how different foods affect you.

Some people do an allergy test where they totally eliminate several food items, and then slowly, one at a time, reintroduce individual items to really get clear feedback on how each one affects their body. Thus allowing truly personal intelligent choices on what foods to eat or avoid. Be willing to try new and different things, and do not give up until you feel healthy and free! Free from that incessant noise in your head about how you wish your body was different and better. Become a healthy version of You, and watch as the noise dissipates. Every trip to the closet does not have to be a battle. Getting dressed should not feel like a war zone each time, where the beat up and wounded is YOU.

You would be surprised by how different my dietary choices are today than say 10–20 years ago. If you would have told me back then about some of the things I eat today, or that I don't eat anymore, I would have felt completely overwhelmed. Too much to consider! I'm not sure I would have felt I had the fortitude to be so much better in this regard. Fast food, anyone? Yet here I am: healthier and as fit as I've ever been. Less getting sick and less aches and pains, despite middle age and the barrage of negative symptoms that aging often implies for many women. This is why I suggest slow and steady, incremental changes. You can choose where you start, and what the changes are. This will increase the likelihood that the changes will become life-style habits that stick around as opposed to dramatic changes that are unsustainable long term. When you take the time to learn what works for you, you will feel a positive difference, and that is when it becomes sustainable.

Additionally, when working out is part of your routine, you will find you want to eat foods that help you recover, and that fuel you for tomorrow's workout. It will not feel like a sacrifice to skip the french fries and chocolate cake because you know healthier food will reward you with feeling better and more energy tomorrow. Then when you do enjoy the french fries and chocolate cake, they will feel like a really special treat! You might enjoy the experience of eating them even more. Or sometimes, with some less-than-healthy foods, like chips and candy, you find you lose the desire for them as your body and taste buds become accustomed to cleaner, more nutrient-dense foods. Either way, if your taste buds change or not, exercise contributes to you finding a nutritional track that serves you better!

The great thing about this subject is that you get a fresh chance to try every single day. Failed epically today? I have those days too! We can do better tomorrow. Every good decision in regard to exercise and nutrition is not a sacrifice, but rather, an investment. You deserve it. You deserve to give your body activities that it is designed to do and that feel fun. You deserve to fuel yourself in a way that serves you. This, too, is a commitment that benefits you and all those who love you. When you feel better more often, you can engage more fully, participate in the game, the sport, the kids' activities, in life. You will find you even have more mental stamina in the office.

Shift your mindset in this way. You are not exercising and eating healthier merely to fit in a certain dress size, or to get the attention of a man; you are doing these things so you can actually LIVE your life! Remember in the beginning, I declared I wanted to know how to "LIVE MY LIFE TO THE FULLEST?" Fitness and nutrition play a key role in the ability to do just that! And, I promise, if you hate _____ (whatever "health" food you do not like), you do not have to eat it!!! Or the same with activity: if you hate _____ (whatever specific kind of exercise you don't like), you do not have to do that! There are a myriad of ways to get the nutrition you need and a myriad of ways to build fitness. You can find your way around those personal preferences and find what your taste buds and your body do love and enjoy those things!

As a personal nutrition example, I cannot enjoy herbal tea. I know it is supposed to be very good for you. I've tried so many, but I don't like the way they make me feel. I always feel worse after drinking herbal teas. So guess what? I don't drink them. But if you love them and they soothe you or soothe your digestion or whatever else they are supposed to do, by all means, you should enjoy herbal tea! Every drop of it! I encourage you to find these things. Both the ones that don't work for you (at least for the time being) and the ones that you absolutely enjoy the taste and the benefit of. Don't just take the word of some "expert." You are the best expert of your own body!

Your effort for physical vitality through exercise and nutrition is by no means a quest for perfection. It is a quest for excellence. It serves as an opportunity for you to know and care for your Self in this life-time—you caring for yourself in a way that no one else can. When you put your head on the pillow at night, and you know that you did your best that day, it yields an internal satisfaction. This does not quench the unquenchable attribute of perfection; this quenches the quench-able attribute of progress, contributing greatly to your inner peace.

All spiritual and physical effort toward growth creates an intrinsic sense of fulfillment. If you are a person who has participated in some spiritual practices, but neglected your physical vessel in the past, by seeking the exercise, nutrition and other physical well-being prac-tices that enhance your life, you will absolutely be able to increase your zen! You may be surprised by the amount of additional zen you experience by adding care of your physical self to your list of priori-ties in your life!

When you do the work consistently to gain optimal vitality, you will still notice the whining and the trash talk coming at you from your ego mind—coming at you from other people or the world—but instead of buckling under it or feeling the need to retaliate, you will be able to stand firm. You will be able to allow the untruths to pass around you, or over you as you are steadfast on your path forward. You will find you are now moving with the authentic strength of You. There is nothing like this feeling. This exemplifies your zen. There will be no question that you are on your right path. Keep doing the work, one stitch at a time in the fabric of the tapestry of your life. A beautiful, unmatched masterpiece awaits you!

Sometimes if you struggle with these practices of fitness or nutrition, there is an underlying reason. Maybe your knee hurts so you don't want to run? Maybe your hormones are unbalanced which creates intense food cravings? This is where we explore additional health and wellness practices. Practices to support you getting on a healthy track and feeling good or staying on a healthy track once you are there.

There are many modalities available to address health issues that may be preventing you from pursuing your best physical self. This is not to serve as medical advice, but to inform you of wellness practices you may not have been aware of, or may not have tried yet. Do not hesitate to investigate and try new things that have the possibility of supporting your body on its search for recovery or equilibrium. Do not stagnate, allowing that ego mind to keep you from improving. Do not say, *This is the way it is, and the way it will always be*! Seek out answers and solutions for yourself.

Begin by getting your blood work and hormone levels checked. If you have physical pain, try chiropractic or acupuncture. Try physical therapy, massage, active-release technique, or cryotherapy. These therapies can tend to existing ailments, and possibly alleviate or manage the pain associated with them. If you do not have an injury or chronic pain, these practices can support your health and fitness journey by keeping or even improving your muscle and joint mobility, or in the case of acupuncture or cryotherapy, by taking down inflammation. As you've heard already so many times, find what works for YOU. Find what can facilitate healing or act as preventive measures for the health of your muscles and joints in the long haul. As a bonus, most of these treatments feel really good!

Louise Hay published some fascinating work about how physical symptoms have a spiritual or emotional component as a root cause. According to Hay and others, if you can make that association, *You Can Heal Your Life* (the title of her most acclaimed book). Dealing with a physical ailment? Consider how thoughts and experiences may have contributed to the less-than-optimal environment in your body. In his book *Biology of Belief*, scientist Bruce Lipton, PhD explains how it has been scientifically proven that our thoughts and our beliefs affect the actual cell membranes that make up our body and each different organ system. These teachings are yet another way to look at spiritual and emotional components intertwining with our physical bodies. Further validating that incorporating our physical body into our spiritual work is essential to achieving the zen in high heels we aspire to. If we accept this research of Lipton, Hay, and others such as Joe Dispenza *Becoming Supernatural*, Karol Kuhn *Feelings Buried Alive Never Die*, and Bessel van der Kolk, MD *The Body Keeps the Score* as true, all the work we did in previous chapters must have a profound and positive effect on our physical bodies. This may not be a connection you have made before. You may never have considered your inflexibility of looking at other or opposing sides of an argument may have contributed to the inflexibility you experience in your neck. Whoa! Can this be so?

These spiritual teachers and scientists alike suggest that all physical ailments stem from an emotional origin. Our bodies create disease because our spirits are in a state of *dis-ease*. If you are having a difficult time releasing something or someone, you may experience constipation. Feeling pissed off? This may manifest as a bladder problem. Can't get anyone to listen to you? This may develop a physical symptom in your throat. Hay declares throat issues may be the result of feeling an inability to speak up, of feeling your voice is being stifled. The energy of such feelings then manifests over time with a physical symptom to get our attention.

The list of ailments and possible emotional associations goes on. If you are new to this concept, research more about it. I am not trying to convince you of anything here. I am introducing the fact that there is scientific research offering loads of studies and reports that support the idea that we—most likely unconsciously—contribute to our body's ability to get sick and/or to get well. This does not negate the role of or need for medical attention or intervention, but rather offers a possible avenue whereby we may be proactive partners with our doctors and our bodies as opposed to absolute helpless bystanders without power or contribution.

Do your own research; you will find that there are many spiritual teachers and scientists who believe that physical ailments can be traced back to an origin of repressed, unexpressed emotions. It is fascinating! Maybe your shoulder pain is a result of feeling that you are carrying the heavy burdens of life on your shoulders?

The point of this knowledge for our purpose here is not to put blame or guilt on ourselves for perhaps creating an internal environment where our physical ailments have been able to manifest. Rather, our purpose is to take a moment to look at illness or undesired symptoms with a new lens of, *If my thoughts or emotions are possibly a contributor, can I recognize ways I may have emotionally or otherwise created energy blocks for myself?* And more importantly, to connect with the concept and the possibility then that if this is not merely a random or solely genetically inherited condition, if we contributed in any way to the illness, wouldn't that make it equally as possible that with changes, we could contribute to our healing? Can we make the decision moving forward to support the physical process of healing by directing our thoughts and emotions toward positivity and hope? Are we willing to take an honest look at things we may be suppressing? Can we address past hurts and trauma, ultimately healing whatever ails us?

If this is too much to consider, how anything you have done or are thinking is causing the sudden bout of heartburn, for instance, don't shoot the messenger! Whatever you believe or do not believe about this topic, I would be remiss in not offering the information and to say if you feel like you've exhausted other medical or non-medical therapies without resolve on an ailment, research the mind-body connection and see if there are solutions for you there. I do believe as you work your way through the earlier spiritual growth principles we covered, that you will notice physically you feel better. Certainly this is true for me. It's hard to believe that in my 20's I felt the need to take ibuprofen almost daily because of back pain. These days, I may take one or two anti-inflammatory pills in a year! My back rarely ever bothers me! As an athletic person, I do chiropractic care for maintenance, and love a hot Epsom salt bath, but I do not use these modalities to ease pain, rather to honor and soothe my active body.

To find wellness or enhance your level of wellness, additional long-standing practices that support the well-being of our physical vessel include: earthing, sunlight, Epsom bath, sauna/hot yoga, neti pot, colonic, dry skin brush, flossing and detoxing personal space and personal care products. No single practice is going to be a miracle of healing or wellness. Living in the 21st century is a life filled with toxicity in our air, our water, our consumer products and our exposure to electromagnetic fields. So it is not about ten minutes of this or a teaspoon of that to cure all that ails us. It is a matter of supporting yourself and your body in as many ways as possible on any given day. "Stressed souls need the reassuring rhythm of self-nurturing rituals," says Sarah ban Breathnach in *Simple Abundance.*

EARTHING. Also referred to as grounding. Clint Ober, author of *Earthing*, is a modern day pioneer, bringing our awareness to the fact that we rarely ever let our bare skin touch the earth. Always in shoes, always indoors—going barefoot, standing barefoot on the earth, the sand, the dirt, hopefully on your chemical-free yard, puts us in touch with the grounding effects of Mother Earth's electromagnetic field to undo some of the overstimulation from electromagnetic frequency exposure of our modern world. This practice harmonizes our root chakra. We become energetically grounded and connected to the earth. Proponents of Earthing claim it can:

- reduce free radicals in our bodies
- neutralize the bombardment of positive ions from our overly chemical and overly electronic environment (negative ions are good for your body and health)

- reduce pain
- help with sleep
- help reduce feelings of stress

Especially after a flight, I now make the effort, weather permitting, to find some grass and put my bare feet on it. Even five minutes grounds me. I make the effort to put my feet on the earth as many days as I can.

Research more about it! Try it! Benefit from this simple, free wellness practice!

SUNLIGHT. There is so much talk of SPF, and "don't forget the sunscreen" that we have forgotten that natural sunshine is important, actually critical to our health! Direct sunlight to part of our skin without sunscreen for only 5–15 minutes can provide these benefits:

- improved immunity
- improved Vitamin D levels and Vitamin D synthesis
- reduced feelings of stress
- stimulate serotonin—boosting mood and alertness (try putting your face to the sun for a couple of minutes, eyes closed of course, to let it affect your brain if you are feeling sluggish)
- is even said to improve the microbiome in our gut

Parts of the planet with less sun exposure have a higher incidence of certain cancers.

Research more about it! Try it! Benefit from this simple, free wellness practice!

EPSOM BATH. A hot bath fortified with Epsom salt is one of my favorite go-to wellness practices! Don't be afraid to use a lot of salt (3 or more cups) in your Epsom bath for benefits such as:

- relaxation of the muscles and nervous system, reducing feelings of stress
- ease of post-workout soreness
- replenishment of magnesium if your body needs it
- improved sleep
- possible relief from minor constipation
- reduced feelings of stress

Research more about it! Try it! Benefit from this simple, low-cost wellness practice!

SAUNA/HOT YOGA. Nothing like a really good sweat! The high temperatures associated with a sauna or hot yoga class heat up the core body temperature. Regular participation has been shown to reduce the risk of all cardiac incidents. Sweating like this is detoxifying. Benefits of incorporating sauna or hot yoga sweating into your routine include:

- aids in exercise recovery
- aids in age-related brain health (Alzheimer's Association)
- may improve deep sleep
- reduces feelings of stress

Research more about it! Try it! Benefit from sweating!

NETI POT (Nasal Irrigation). Sinus irrigation with salt water can ease symptoms of allergy season. People who suffer numerous sinus infections throughout the year may benefit from regular Neti pot use. This practice:

- Might save you from needing to take antibiotics for recurring sinus infections
- Can save you from needing to suffer through seasonal allergies. Either acting as a replacement for allergy medication, or as a supporting practice for your allergy medication.
- Is said to clear germs, bacteria and viruses from your nasal cavity, which could be helpful after exposure to large groups of people, or sick people, or after a long day of travel—rinse them out to reduce their impact on your body
- Will clear your nasal pathway when fighting a cold, allowing you to clear mucus more than just Kleenex blowing, and allowing you to breathe better to get your rest.

Research more about it! Try it! Benefit from this simple, low-cost wellness practice!

COLONIC. When I first heard of colonic therapy about 20 years ago, I cringed! *You put a tube where? And you do what?!* As someone who has never struggled with constipation, I just couldn't imagine WHY I should consider getting a professional colonic. But my friend who told me about it raved about the benefits she experienced, so I did my research. I was fascinated to learn that before the pharmaceutical industry was a thing, doctors used to treat sick patients by tending to the colon. The colon was intricately linked with health and immunity. As I mentioned earlier, anything I could do to support immunity, I was willing to try!

It does make sense that getting rid of any old, possibly toxic poop from the porous walls of the large intestine would free you up for better absorption of food nutrients and might facilitate a myriad of other benefits. You can decide for yourself if you feel a benefit. You can get a colonic once a year, maybe after the holiday splurges, or maybe seasonally as a detox support. Or anytime you have a health issue and you want to support your immune system. It is another alternative therapy you can tailor to your needs. Benefits of colonic therapy are said to include:

- detoxification support
- improved immune function
- clearer skin and clearer thoughts
- as an aid to your spiritual and emotional work of clearing things you've been unnecessarily holding on to

Research it! Try it! Benefit from this 45–60 minute session of ridding your colon of any built-up toxins or debris!

DRY SKIN BRUSH. Consider adding dry skin brushing into your daily routine. Or maybe just add it to the days you will sweat in a sauna or hot yoga class. Allow the perspiration to escape freely, not get trapped under some dead skin cells! Benefits of dry skin brushing are said to include:

- lymphatic stimulation
- exfoliation of the skin, revealing softer skin over time
- possible increased circulation and energy boost
- stimulation to possibly minimize areas of cellulite

Research it! Try it! Benefit from this quick and low-cost practice!

FLOSSING. Your dentist tells you this at every checkup! Leave your floss out for the first couple of weeks until it becomes a habit. Once it does, you will not be able to go to bed without flossing! Flossing leaves your mouth feeling cleaner than brushing alone can. A growing body of evidence has linked oral health particularly periodontal (gum) disease to several chronic diseases including diabetes, heart disease and stroke. Schedule regular dental checkups, and floss! Benefits of nightly flossing include:

- reduced risk for gum disease
- fresher breath
- reduced risk for heart disease
- chance of fewer cavities

Research the benefits! Try it! Make flossing a nighttime habit for good oral and heart health!

DETOX personal care products and personal space. Opinions vary as to how toxic the chemicals in our cosmetic, bath and house cleaning products are. Or how many pesticides and toxins are in our food, our water, and the air we breathe. And opinions vary as to how much our human bodies can tolerate such chemicals. But what is not controversial, is the fact that we are exposed to toxic chemicals everywhere we turn! There would be no way of eliminating this part of our life experience in today's world, but we can assume responsibility in small ways to reduce or minimize exposure. Look up the benefit of vinegar as a cleaning product and shop for cleaning, cosmetic and bath products that are specifically formulated with organic or natural ingredients. Maybe get an air purifier in your bedroom and a water purifier on your kitchen faucet or shower. Buy local or organic produce. There are many ways we can clean up our personal space and personal exposure to toxins. As part of wellness practice for your health and well-being, this is something you won't want to overlook.

Research the benefits! Try it! Make living cleaner a priority for yourself!

This is by no means a complete or comprehensive list of all alternative wellness practices. These are ones that are relatively easy and very practical. These are practices I am familiar with, and ones that have made an undeniable difference in supporting my personal health. Additional practices you can research and try might include things like a daily stretch routine, specific breath work or aromatherapy with essential oils. Be open to trying new things and the big takeaway point is for each of us to take personal responsibility and accountability for our overall health and wellness and appreciate all the ways such actions positively contribute to our lives. If you do not educate yourself and get proactive with your own well-being, then who will? No one else will—that is the problem, the challenge, the responsibility—the honor, really.

What I hope you got out of this chapter is that taking care of your body is more than just trying to fit into a bikini on vacation. We add INTENTION to our workout and nutrition and health practice choices. We wisely choose to be active and choose what foods to eat with the intention of showing up for our lives and for the people in our lives. We become more and more healthy through the years as we listen to our body and learn how it communicates what it needs. Nurturing this relationship enhances not just the image in the mirror, but our everyday existence. I hope you are looking at this relationship and your choices now through this broadened spiritual lens! A well-cared-for spirit deserves a well-cared-for vessel in which it gets to explore life and express itself! Be well.

PART V

Tying It All Together

CHAPTER 15

Fluidity

"Don't try to force a square peg in a round hole."

—SYDNEY SMITH

*L*ife is fluid. Emotions are fluid. I propose allowing the solutions you seek for your life to be fluid as well. One of the things that makes *Zen in High Heels* different is that I encourage you to combine, or interchange when necessary the principles that I share. This is a critical component in my opinion of successful implementation of any or all of the principles. For most of us, none of the practices are *always* the answer in every circumstance or with every person. These principles are not mutually exclusive. You do not have to pick and choose which ONE works for you. We can use many of the different tools at different times along our way.

I present these principles with the stipulation that this is not a step-by-step guide. Some principles are more easily applied now, some later. Some issues require more of *this*, some issues need more of *that*. This also allows the principles to have a synergistic effect when applied together. Each tool offers a different perspective, often revealing stepping stones for you as you seek to find a better way.

Personal growth principles are interlinked to some degree. This is such an important thing to know! This concept of fluidity has been paramount on my journey of growth! Approaching your spiritual evolution from this perspective is not anything I have read before and not something I have had explained to me. It was this realization that I had through trial and error that really propelled me as I struggled with that original dilemma of knowing the qualities I longed for in my life, but not knowing how to actually live them without constantly getting derailed by "real" life.

Eckhart Tolle, for example, teaches primarily: do not be caught up in the past, or in the future, but BE PRESENT. For it is IN THIS MOMENT only that peace and zen reside. Great. Being present would always make any given situation better. No doubt. And being present is the goal of a spiritually enlightened person. But there are some moments along my journey where I am not present. But because I'm engaged on my spiritual path, I am aware that I am not present. I cannot seem to find presence in a particular circumstance or with a certain person. Can I keep trying and trying and keep practicing and eventually get there? Probably. But why not try to apply other principles to this stubborn scenario in the meantime? This is where I get out another tool from my spiritual toolbox and apply it. This other tool may soften my stance just enough or give me the revelation I need so I am then able to come back around and find the presence I seek.

Another example, Don Miguel Ruiz teaches the principle of non-attachment. Yes, any circumstance would be better from a position of non-attachment. True, a spiritually enlightened person would not be unhealthily attached to any outside person, thing, circumstance or outcome for their sense of peace or happiness. But on occasion, I cannot seem to "unattach" myself from said person, thing, circumstance or outcome I desire. I seem to care too much, or my ego may be too invested in this particular situation. The spiritual wrench called non-attachment doesn't seem to fit here at this time for me. I'll try a different tool.

Same with the Law of Attraction. Maybe it does work. Maybe it is the answer. But right now, dear Law of Attraction, my life is a shit show. I will choose to think positive and "manifest" until it changes and look at ways I may have attracted this problem to me, but what about in the meantime? I need another tool TODAY! I cannot positive think and visualize the feeling of wealth to get myself out of bankruptcy court tomorrow.

So try as you may, applying one particular principle to a situation you are going through may not yield the results you seek. This is not to imply that a spiritual principle is not applicable or effective or true 100% of the time. If we were a master at the principle, it would no doubt work. This is to say that because we are not yet masters, but still learning and growing and trying and have a long way to go, we may find we experience a block or a blindspot when trying to apply a particular principle to a particular difficult situation. Based on our life history and our emotional landscape, some ways of dealing with issues may click easier for us than others.

My hope is that in times when you feel derailed or stuck, you will understand that it is normal. It is part of the process. Finding yourself in a situation where you feel like you've hit a brick wall is nothing to beat yourself up about. Just because one principle worked on one of your other problems, does not negate the value of other principles for other problems. It can be frustrating. I hope understanding the idea of tools in your toolbox can be a very practical way to apply these principles in your life TODAY! Not *someday* when you get it all figured out. Key point: spirituality is fluid and expansive, not constrictive and dependent on one way of resolution. *If "x" does not work, you've done something wrong, and you are screwed.* NO! Do not stay discouraged. Broaden your outlook and try a different angle.

Do not give up! Finding the right principle to apply at the right time yields a breakthrough of growth and understanding. For example, the practice of presence may allow the space to finally let go of the attachment. One principle allowed you to build or break through to another principle. This opens up possibilities you didn't see or experience before. This reiterates the point that growth is possible from EXACTLY WHERE YOU ARE. You do not have to wait until you are in a better mood, or feel more spiritual. Acknowledge honestly where you are, and make decisions from there. Do as any quality handyman would do: pull out the tool that works for the situation at hand.

I have not shared any principles in *Zen in High Heels* that I have merely read about, and in theory, I think should work. Every single principle, concept or piece of advice actually has worked for me, and changed my life. Although when I began my journey of seeking, it was a subtle pull toward finding more meaning, as I grew and as time passed, life threw some real doozies at me—as it does for all of us.

At some time or another, we all have to go through a fire. We will all be tested. It is in the experiencing of such major life shifts that we come to see who we are and what we are made of. It is SO vital not to question, *Why me?* Imagine as you are incarnated into physical form, your soul understands that it will be a necessary part of your human experience to overcome what seem like tragic blows, to survive what seems like certain demise. It's true for every single person. Albeit the tragedies are different, they serve the purpose of testing and teaching us. Tragedies fragment the structure of the ego and give us a chance to see beyond its protective but false veil. If we will allow the wisdom and the grace buried in difficult, even impossible circumstances to actually propel us forward on our journey of evolution, we will ultimately live better and feel more alive than ever.

My trial by fire began in 2003 as I found myself trying to make my way out of an enveloping darkness after the traumatic delivery experience of my daughter being born and the subsequent postpartum depression. The fire continued in the soon after revelation of cracks in my once happy marriage that unexpectedly and devastatingly led to its collapse. It was topped off with the death of my 39-year-old stepbrother in a tragic auto accident on a sunny summer Monday, just before his son was to start kindergarten. These experiences gave me reason to put every principle to the test.

It took a long while—I'm talking years—but I was determined not to numb or distract myself as I tried to find my way out of the darkness. I was determined to make sense of it all. I was determined to learn every last drop of wisdom and understanding that those experiences had for me, to give my life more meaning, and when I found the light again, to not be carrying the heavy metaphorical load of the pain each had instilled upon me. Rather, I allowed the experiences and the deep pain attached to them to help me see more clearly things that before then were un-see-able to me. Each of these events changed me. All happening within a ten-year span.

There was a time during the fire that I felt debilitated. Maybe not obvious on the outside, but inside I was crippled. Not knowing some moments if I could make it to the next breath. And thinking that if the next breath was going to feel anything like the last breath, maybe I did not even want to. The life I was experiencing and the thoughts I was thinking were unrecognizable to me. I was in an emotional and spiritual tornado. The sunny dispositioned, overachieving, type A woman I once embodied was struggling for survival. The only thing I knew was that if God has given me another day, He must have a purpose for me that I could not yet see, and that I was going to live through the fire. I had a deep, steadfast conviction to honor Him, and to honor my brother, and be an honorable mother to my daughter.

I was forced to learn to embrace Deepak Chopra's teaching to "make peace with uncertainty." And, as uncertainty is always fundamentally a quality of life in varying degrees, the peace in and around uncertainty remains with me. I don't worry about anything. I continue to practice the principles and use the filter of the wisdom they instilled in me for every part of my life. I have experienced deep and lasting growth and inner peace. My life is profoundly better in every way that matters to me. Yours can be too.

Trust the wisdom that has been around for centuries. Experiment with how and where these spiritual principles can be applied in the context of your personal life. Your understanding of and use of these tools will allow you to experience peace and freedom. This will enable YOU to show up and engage fully in your life! Zen will be yours!

CHAPTER 16

The World Needs You

"Self-growth is tender, it's holy ground. There's no greater investment."

—STEPHEN R. COVEY

You may wonder or ask, *what about the spiritual ideation that we are lovable just as we are? That we have nothing to prove to be lovable? And to be happy with what IS. How do we reconcile this with all the work and challenges you are asking us to do?* The answer is simple. Just as you love your child, no matter what they do or do not do, nothing can take away that love. You will always love them. Your love and acceptance of them are unconditional, this is true. Also, it is in the divine manner, that we who unconditionally love our child want them to use that stability and personal security as a jumping point.

We want them to feel safe and secure enough to grow, to expand and to find their potential in this lifetime.

We honor the divine and we honor the gift of our time on earth by digging and forging our way even when things do not appear easy, to find what we are made of. It is in the process of seeking and removing the blocks on our path, that our strength is revealed. These experiences teach us who we are on the inside. Irrespective of who our parents are or who we appear to be in society, we come to know our truth and subsequently our purpose.

It is in the challenges that life presents, and in seeking understanding during those challenges, that we are able to expand and grow. I can understand that I am OK right where I am, exactly as I am. I am lovable. And, from there, I will strive, or better said, THRIVE toward my ultimate potential! Believing that I am loved and lovable actually allows me to extend myself emotionally and physically to expand and evolve to be available for the call that life has for me. I must be willing to grow. I must seek growth in order to evolve.

Thankfully it is not a dichotomy to accept yourself for who and where you are today, but also believe there is room to change and improve. You can acknowledge that the circumstances and the emotional tools you've had access to up to this point in life have led you to exactly where you are. I can love and accept myself today but not let past or current circumstances or lack of tools up to this point limit me and my ability to flourish into a better version of myself tomorrow. *I accept myself today AND I believe there is room for change and improvement.* We are not meant to spend a lifetime in struggle. However, striving toward our innate potential is natural and DNA-instructed. Just observe nature. The seed of a fruit tree does not achieve its potential or its ability to serve the world with the fruit it bears by remaining a seed.

Our destiny awaits if we are willing to do the spiritual, emotional and physical work. It comes with great reward. Growing and being conscious is a privilege. It is not all difficulty and drudgery. Exploring and pushing our current self or society-imposed boundaries of who we can be, results in expansion. Expansion is where you will find peace and freedom. We then become available. We can then show up and give the gift of ourselves. Truly.

No one benefits from you hiding. Again, the afraid, defensive, unaccountable, codependent, insecure, maybe out-of-shape and sick version of You is still as deserving of love as anyone else. It is your choice to be proactive in your growth or not. You can skate and skirt the issues and the responsibilities life presents you. You can. And you will still be worthy of love, you will. But the impact you could have, and the unused gifts you could have given to this world will go unexpressed and unrealized. If you choose this route, the unique divinely appointed gifts that you were meant to share in your lifetime, will be buried with you when you die.

A chaotic life, or any signs of restlessness, or inner turmoil are just indicators that your spiritual path awaits you. Your journey of discovery is waiting for your attention and your participation. It is a personal call. It is personal work. It may seem scary, it may seem exciting, it may be both. I know with 100% certainty that you can do it. You will be presented with the teachers, the tools and the support you need if you are honest and pure in your intention. What you will find on the other side of this work, will be worth the pursuing of it.

There are ebbs and flows. You can put your attention on and solve and resolve a re-occurring issue in your life once and for all, and grow from there. Then you can enjoy the fruits of that growth for a season or two, until the next big challenge presents itself, or knocks on your soul to tend to. It is beautiful like the waves.

The work presented in *Zen in High Heels* is very powerful. If you choose to embrace it and consciously embark on your own journey of discovery, you will no doubt see transformation in your life. Along the way, it can feel dark and confusing. There are times you may feel very alone. The most profound moments of clarity and truth for you and about you come from spending time alone. Well, you will find you are not actually alone. You will find you are actually WITH your Self and with your Creator. The space of deep self-discovery is a space designed for no other humans to fit into it with you. There is just enough room in the darkness for you and your God. When you are honest and open on your quest of seeking truth for yourself, divinity is there to guide you. This is often referred to as the dark night of the soul. It is, as far as I can tell, a necessary part of the process.

You are not meant to stay in the places of darkest darkness for long. There is only enough oxygen there for you to get what you need, and get out. Surrender and let go of the need for a definitive timeline or what the outcome must look like. Trust the process and know that you will emerge on the other side with a renewed and more accurate sense of Self and with a knowledge of your own strength. This is a self-discovered, self-earned strength that no one else can bestow upon you. No one can give it to you, and no one can take it from you. You will have uncovered, discovered and experienced your own strength. This knowing of your truth and your strength is the foundation on which you will stand and grow into your well-deserved space of zen. It is the most authentically powerful place from which you can operate. Your journey of growth and subsequent wisdom that comes with it, creates a fearlessness. You will no longer fear being seen. You will no longer fear the disapproval of others. You will no longer fear being You.

However, if you do not learn who you are in those dark moments, if you choose rather to run from or numb yourself instead of seeking the wisdom they offer, you will find the foundation on which you stand in the light of who you believe yourself to be is based only on assumptions. Assumptions that you have made about yourself or assumptions others have made about you are never fully accurate or encompassing of your actual truth. A lack of deep spiritual work on oneself is what causes many who seem strong in the light to eventually crumble. The disparity between who they are and who they are pretending to be is too vast. That disparity creates a feeling of inescapable darkness in which they are unable to see the light at the end of the tunnel. This is the beginning of an existential crisis.

In addition to those few times in life that involve isolation and seeming darkness, I hope you have learned in *Zen in High Heels* that spiritual growth is waiting for you in everyday moments. Spiritual growth is found in the moment of not picking up the phone in a reactionary state to gossip or carry on about the latest family or neighborhood drama. Growth is found in the moment that you catch yourself, and choose not to speak the half-truth. Personal growth occurs in the moment you choose not to have your cell phone at the dinner table, but instead to be present and connect with those you are blessed to be dining with. It is in this awareness–your spiritual evolution is in each moment of new awareness when you make the decision that is better for You.

Choosing the decision that represents your truth breeds evolution. It is beautiful when you are living this way. Profound and meaningful occurrences can happen at any time—on any ordinary day: a Tuesday in April for example! You can experience your zen waiting in line at a crowded restaurant—or anywhere else for that matter!

Life is about change and progress. Well, change for sure, progress is up to you. Deepak says, "growth is the willingness to let each moment be new." This is so profound, if we could really live our lives this way. When we bring a version of ourselves that is open to allowing each moment the permission and the possibility to be different or new, circumstances of our lives become an endless opportunity for revelation and discovery! Despite previous or anticipated outcomes and despite any evidence of it turning out any differently than it ever has before, with our faith and open-mindedness, things change.

People might show up differently than we anticipated because of our willingness to allow the possibility of them to do so. We might gain new insights. Truth has a chance to reveal itself to us, and we have a chance to see it! Change becomes possible. All things become possible. There is a freedom in not being limited by our preconceived notions.

Understand that what we think we know, is always only based on what we have learned up to this point. Growth is in the unknown, in the openness of what might be. With our growth, comes expansion. Expansion is living. No matter how old we are, life becomes the fascinating journey it is meant to be! All of this starts with conscious awareness. When you are ready and willing to observe your life, you will get somewhere. No more being stuck.

Growth requires truth. All the good stuff happens when you stop hiding from the truth. That drama in your life is not *Who* you are. So stop talking about it. Words are fuel. Do not put your words into a fire that you do not desire to burn bigger. You get to decide it's enough already! Stop justifying any habit or unhealthy relationship pattern that is causing you pain. Be courageous enough to stop the denial, to stop the blame. Stop the denial, the blame and the justification in the words you speak to others and, most importantly, in the words you speak to YOU.

Move yourself toward resolution. Deal with what needs to be dealt with, and do not focus on the turmoil around you as your gauge. Keep making the right decisions. *In this moment, am I contributing to the turmoil or to peace?* Let intention and integrity drive you. Figure out who you are and let the intention and integrity of your desires, your words and your actions lead you forward. Get off the re-action train as a passenger.

As you seek enlightenment, may the practice of these principles presented in *Zen in High Heels* put your mind at ease. May you find less worry, because you now know that there is no reason to worry. You now realize that you only have control over what it is you have control over, and that is enough. Seek the love, not the fear.

Personal growth is always for the better. Your personal growth will give you a better understanding of your journey. You will have more compassion for yourself and for others and more ability to understand how to find your own happiness and satisfaction. Only good things come with growth. Often what it takes to get there does not feel good, but where you end up, is always, always better than where you began.

> *"When we finally have a glimpse of our own completion as human beings—regardless of our husband or lack of one, our boyfriend or lack of one, our job or lack of one, our money or lack of it, our children or lack of any, or whatever else we think we need in order to thrive and be happy. When we have finally touched on a spiritual high that is real and enduring, then we know that the pain of getting there was worth it."*

> —MARIANNE WILLIAMSON, *A WOMAN'S WORTH*

It was with the principles and practices laid out in these chapters that I discovered the answer to my initial question of what was missing in my life. What I learned, and what I now understand, is that what my life actually needed more of, was ME. I was what was missing! I felt internal conflict because I could not fully be me. But that was my responsibility. Nobody else can define me (or you). Only I can discover for myself WHO I am, and decide how I want to show up. Only I can discover the obstacles and blocks that are present in my life, keeping me from actualizing my zen. It's a very personal journey. It's an adventure, really! "Your time is limited, so don't waste it living someone else's life...have the courage to follow your own heart and intuition." Steve Jobs

Every chapter has either said outright, or alluded to the fact that everything about your personal, spiritual evolution begins and ends with YOU. You, You, You! You make the decision, you become aware, you do the work to heal, you practice, you grow. It is your life! It is your response! It is your responsibility! The goal is to get You right with You. That knight in shining armor that we grew up hoping might someday come and rescue us is just a metaphor. The knight is a situation. The shining armor is a mirror. The knight is reflecting You back at You! You must be willing to look at and see YOU. YOU are the answers you seek! And when you understand it this way, it will indeed save you from living a life filled with chaos and despair! Take back your power! Rescue your Self!

You will come to understand that you love yourself by honoring yourself. You honor yourself by making choices that support your soul's truth, choices that support your physical body's ability to be well and thrive. You honor yourself by making choices today that contribute to growth in the direction of your potential. Clarity about what choices will lead to your growth is found in the quiet, private time of meditation, and then it is reinforced and strengthened by experiencing the increase of inner peace and fulfillment that come from those choices. Life feels less tumultuous.

You can celebrate the small victories in your everyday life—that rude clerk did not steal your joyful mood. Getting stuck in traffic did not make your blood boil! You just take a deep breath and think of your gratitude list for the day! A minor rude encounter or a minor inconvenience remains just that: MINOR. Such seemingly small progress makes you happy! You will find satisfaction in these small victories. Your heart will feel fuller! You can feel that you are moving forward on your spiritual path. Ego is less. Spirit is more. And it's all happening while you are wearing your newest favorite lip gloss and your go-to favorite pair of high heels! When you figure out who you are, and figure out how to express the truth of you in your life, zen abounds!

It is my hope that you now see the possibility of living your life with more love, less regret, speaking more truthfully, and acting more authentically. I hope you understand that the quality of the relationship you foster with yourself DIRECTLY affects the quality of the relationships you have with other people. I hope you can appreciate your body for the miracle that it is, and give it more of what it needs to thrive. I hope you realize the finiteness of this experience of life in the infiniteness of the Universe. It is the yin; it is the yang. It is in being present, yet seeking more. More of You. More of your truth.

Zen is that calm, centered, everything is A-OK feeling. Actually, it is more than a feeling, it is a knowing. Zen can express itself spiritually, emotionally or physically. Zen is the opposite of fear, chaos, anger, resentment and anything that stands between you and your peace. It's a state of being where your actions represent your values, resulting in a deep sense of harmony within yourself and within your life. It is in this state that we feel the most loving and the most lovable. We become connected simply, deeply and profoundly to everyone and everything around us. This connection is ALWAYS available, but it is that "zen factor" that allows this ever-present availability into our consciousness.

Zen does not happen like a fireworks explosion. Nor do you look in the mirror one day to see a halo has appeared around your head, proclaiming your enlightened-ness! It is possible that you wake up after months or years of making incremental changes and better choices that your life has a more zen-like quality: less drama, more love, more moments of truthful expression and more moments of deep meaning that feel fulfilling and bring peace to your mind and heart. You must not underestimate the significance of every decision you make in alignment with your deeper, authentic self.

Just as food and daily lifestyle choices add up and have a cumulative effect, so too do daily spiritual life choices: taking time to meditate, being intentional, telling the truth, listening. All of your actions or non-actions are impactful. Just having the consciousness that the things you do and do not do matter, adds a sense of meaning to each day. Daily, even moment-to-moment choices you make, create a momentum in moving you in the direction toward your expanded, evolved, enlightened experience of your life or not.

As you start trusting your Self, you will experience progress. Internal peace begins to find you. Accept that some weeks are better than other weeks, some days are better than other days. Some hours of a day are better than other hours of the same day. It is dependent on so many variables—but ultimately the variables begin and end with You. There is no exception to this rule.

As you progress, you will have more and more good hours in a day, more and more good days in a week and more and more good weeks in a month. You will notice less time is spent being pulled off center, succumbing to outside influences or to the weaker parts of yourself. This is something we can all aspire to, which ultimately results in the joy, the peace and the zen we are seeking.

The benefits of you doing the work and consciously engaging on your spiritual path will far exceed your own life! The benefit is experienced as the availability of You to the people around you. Your ability to engage and be present in your life in big and in small moments will have a positive impact in ways you can't even imagine and in ways you may never even know. The benefits of an evolved life are immeasurable. Your spiritual work and growth have a ripple effect. As your relationship with You gets better, it improves your relationship with your family, your friends and coworkers, your social circle of influence, your community, your state, your country and the world. Healing the world begins with healing your Self.

In doing this evolutionary work, you impact your kids' lives in a way that will impact their primary relationships and their kids' lives. And so on. It is a multigenerational gift! The results of the work laid out in *Zen in High Heels* are your contribution to the world. The world is a better place for it. In finding your way to healing the deep trauma or wounds of your life, you are then able to stand as an example to others of what healing is possible for them also. You become a light in that regard because of your willingness to do the work. Now, you can see your light can illuminate even brighter than an unevolved version of you could ever shine. You become more effective in all the ways you desire to be effective.

Serving others moves way up on the list of priorities in a person who is healed. Even the philanthropic work you engage in will be more impactful when you are volunteering, donating or engaging with an authentically powered YOU. An authentic You is a more impactful You. Reiterating that healing the world begins with each of us healing ourselves.

You expressing yourself wholly and truthfully as often as possible is your real legacy. This work creates a miracle. You become the miracle. The world needs a healed version of you! The world needs You.

Conclusion

"You are under no obligation to be the same person you were five minutes ago."

—ALAN WATTS

I have often thought learning a foreign language would be a fun challenge and a great skill to have. I had a realization when I began reading books and studying about spiritual and personal growth over 30 years ago, that it was indeed very much like a foreign language to me. It was at least a foreign *concept* to me for sure.

I had it all wrong with the incessant thinking, doing and trying, hoping that "someday" an accomplishment or an acknowledgment would finally be the thing to bring the sense of meaning and fulfillment that I was longing for. Maybe *then* I would find serenity and lasting happiness?

The idea that I could actually just BE at any given moment, and that would feel like enough? Whoa! Foreign concept indeed to the type A overachiever that I was! The idea that I could learn to observe my thoughts and my behavior patterns, and adjust them? All by myself? The idea that I had that kind of power in my life? Operating from love and peace could be *MY* M.O.? Initially I was not really convinced that this was actually possible. I was curious though, and I was hungry to learn more. I became a sponge. I became committed to what turned out to be the most important, most rewarding work of my life.

Our truth is 100% light. Like so many things in life, we have to build up our tolerance. Going from mostly darkness, to living in the illumination of our most true Self will take some practice, some getting used to. Acknowledging this is another one of the things that makes *Zen in High Heels* different. I acknowledge that gaining enlightenment is not necessarily a linear path. I acknowledge that it is OK to take baby steps and that it is not failure to step into your light for a moment or a brief time, and then need to retreat back to hiding, or numbing or comfort. Continue your quest and keep testing the water. You will get to the point where your tolerance for truth exceeds your tolerance of continuing to hide. Keep flexing your spiritual muscles, gain strength, and find your way. Just never, ever give up. Never give up on You. Where there is breath, there is hope. Where there is progress, there is growth. It may take a lifetime to rediscover your true, essential self fully and to reveal that version of you to the world. No matter how long it takes, you will find that it was worth it. You are worth it.

Zen in High Heels is not necessarily about the proverbial "having it all." It is about wherever you are in your life, being able to present yourself in a way that feels genuine. *Zen in High Heels* is our imperfect journey. It's about wanting to express the love in your heart on as many days as possible. And, also, it is accepting of times you find yourself in your pajamas, eating raw cookie dough and scrolling Sephora for another new lip gloss, when you need to hit "pause" on the world and all of its demands! *Zen in High Heels* is your journey, and it's mine—filled with hope and possibility, but honesty and compassion for where we fall short. It is not about holding on to peace necessarily 24/7, but about having the tools to support yourself toward that goal.

Zen in High Heels is meant to offer a realistic portrayal of what your zen might look like and feel like, so that you may recognize it when it starts to show up. This work, and work like this, supports us in knowing that we do not have to accept or settle for the way things have *always been*. You are not merely a bystander or spectator for your life. Trust your gut. Use the general set point of your emotions as a clue to whether or not things need to be different. Are the average, normal emotions of your day mostly positive or mostly negative? You have the power to discern, and you have the power to seek the answers to make meaningful and lasting changes. Your life can get better.

We want today and every day to see an expanded—versus restricted—version of YOU! When someone asks, "How are you?" You will be able to honestly respond, "I am a better, truer version of myself today than I was yesterday! All is well."

We realize that life rarely pauses long enough for us to pool all of our resources to get "it" figured out. But now we have an understanding. *Zen in High Heels* has laid out spiritual and life principles, so now we have an action plan, not merely a wish for things to be better. This process of experiencing the masterpiece of our true Self in this lifetime is not unlike that of Michael Angelo—we must chip away at what does not belong, revealing in time exactly what we need to allow ourselves to show up as the very best version possible in any given moment.

This work will allow you to bring a better version of yourself to your life and to your loved ones. This is what I want for Me. It is what I want for the people around me. It is what I want for You. Imagine our lives, our neighborhoods and communities where we are operating from this place of each of us striving to communicate in spoken and unspoken ways from the zen we have sought and ultimately can say we found.

Relationships with personal intimate partners and family will have a chance to become stronger and healthier. When you bring an honest, healed version of you, a version of you who meets her own deepest needs and allows others the space to do the same for themselves, you create an environment of trust, an environment that welcomes vulnerability. You get a chance to see and be seen, resulting in the meaning and connection that fill your heart and satisfy your soul. Nothing material, and no amount of money hold the value of this evolved version of you being expressed in your lifetime.

In the truest sense, you are most effective and shine your light the brightest for others only when you yourself are whole and healed.

Only then can you leave the meaningful, impactful imprint on the lives of others as you desire. You may rest in your final days, knowing God can whisper in your ear, "Well done my good and faithful servant." (Matthew 25:21) You will have lived YOUR life, which is what you came here to do.

Now that you are familiar with all of the principles, I can sum up what I hope you have learned as this: improving your life, experiencing all of the qualities you long for, achieving that zen in those high heels, involves understanding and always coming back to your point of power. Your point of power is YOU. Your point of power is NOW. By taking these two things and enveloping them in gratitude and intention, your life will change in ways you have only dared to dream might be possible. Recurring problems or recurring drama will find resolution with this equation in action. It is the most beautiful thing, to know this is true for you. You will create discipline by understanding and desiring what decisions are truly best for you. You will create resilience by testing past or current circumstances through the lens of intention. You will create the healing your heart and soul long for as you tend to your own needs. Bliss is not measured from the outside. Do this, plus that, and you will achieve Nirvana. No, rather, it is about you being a better version of You and then you experiencing the ways your life blossoms because of that growth!

You are enough. Settle down and get to work. Get to know your truth. Begin acting in alignment with her, integrate your thoughts, words and actions, and you will come to know: ALL IS WELL.

Thank you for taking the deep, deep dive of *Zen in High Heels* with me! If you've been familiar with and working with some of the principles already in your life, I hope you found that the chapters are laid out in a way that allowed you to weave some of those familiar principles together in a meaningful, yet very practical, way—putting some of the pieces of the puzzle together for you. If this is your first time hearing many of these principles, congratulations! It is my desire that the insights have expanded your awareness, and that you found the tools laid out in a way that illustrate avenues to explore and practical steps to take as you begin your personal growth into consciousness. I hope you now see the many, many ways you can reclaim your power to make your life better. May you now realize the undeniable possibility that tomorrow can be better than yesterday!

I offer *Zen in High Heels* to you as my gift of support during this brief experience we call life. It is my hope that you feel like celebrating the awesome fabulousness that is YOU! Your journey of one leads to unity and compassion and connectedness with everything. You are not alone. As we part ways, I am offering you a spiritual hug. The light that is in me sees and acknowledges the light that is in you. Namaste.

Recommended Reading

A Woman's Worth, Marianne Williamson

Becoming Supernatural: How Common People Are Doing the Uncommon, Joe Dispenza

Can't Hurt Me: *Master Your mind and Defy the Odds*, David Goggins

Earthing: The Most Important Health Discovery Ever!, Clint Ober, Stephen T. Sinatra, and Martin Zucker

Feelings Buried Alive Never Die, Karol K. Truman

Sacred Contracts, Carolyn Myss

Simple Abundance: Awakening Your Divine Potential, Sarah Ban Breathnach

The Biology of Belief: Unleashing the Power of Consciousness, Matter & Miracles, Bruce Lipton

The Body Keeps the Score: Brain, Mind, and Body in the Healing of Trauma, Bessel van der Kolk

The Four Agreements: A Practical Guide to Personal Freedom, Don Miguel Ruiz

The Power of Infinite Love & Gratitude: An Evolutionary Journey to Awakening Your Spirit, Darren R. Weissman

The Power of Intention: Learning to Co-Create Your World Your Way, Wayne W. Dyer

The Power of Now: A Guide to Spiritual Enlightenment, Eckhart Tolle

The Seat of the Soul, Gary Zukav

The Seven Spiritual Laws of Success: A Pocketbook Guide to Fulfilling Your Dreams, Deepak Chopra

The War of Art, Steven Pressfield

You Can Heal Your Life, Louise L. Hay

Made in the USA
Monee, IL
26 June 2023

37631327R00155